Science Concept Cartoons®

Set 2

Written by

Jo Moules, Jo Horlock, Stuart Naylor and Brenda Keogh

Millgate House Education

First published in 2015 by Millgate House Publishers

Millgate House Publishers is an imprint of
Millgate House Education Ltd.
Unit 1, Zan Business Park
Crewe Road
Sandbach
Cheshire
CW11 4QD
UK

www.millgatehouse.co.uk

British Library Cataloguing in Publication Data
A catalogue record for this book is available from the British Library.

ISBN 978-0-9562646-8-8

Graphic design by Neil Pepper and Bill Corrigan
Illustrations by Ged Mitchell and Jo Williams

Printed and bound in Great Britain by Sterling Solutions

This publication is dedicated to the memory of Brenda Keogh,

whose contributions to this book were invaluable. As the creator of

Concept Cartoons, she was delighted to see the impact they have had on

teachers and learners around the world. As with all the earlier

Concept Cartoon publications, her insight, her ideas and her inspiration

have profoundly influenced this latest set. We will treasure her memory,

and we will miss her.

Contents

i.   Acknowledgements

This book (and CD ROM) follows its partner publications, Science Concept Cartoons Set 1 (Naylor and Keogh, 2010), Concept Cartoons in Mathematics (Naylor, Keogh and Dabell, 2008) and English Concept Cartoons (Turner, Smith, Keogh and Naylor, 2014).

We wish to express our grateful thanks to:
· Illustrator Ged Mitchell, whose drawings bring ours ideas to life
· Project manager Jo Williams, whose questions, comments and ideas have been so useful
· Graphic designers Neil Pepper and Bill Corrigan for patiently turning ideas into a reality
· All the teachers who have inspired us to create a second volume

ii.   Essential Information

Each section of the book and CD ROM has support material, with ideas for follow up activities and background information together with extension ideas. All of the background text is written in learner-friendly language.

Concept Cartoons are normally used near the start of a lesson, followed by paired or small group discussion, and then an opportunity to explore or research the ideas being discussed. You do not need long periods of discussion to have an impact on the lesson.

Ask learners to discuss why each character in the Concept Cartoon might hold their particular idea. What might go in the blank speech bubble?

Some Concept Cartoons might initially appear too easy for some learners, but they can provide a useful starting point for discussion about more complex ideas and often reveal some basic misunderstandings. They can also be used with learners who lack confidence or experience in science. If you have the CD ROM you can adjust the level of demand by changing the text.

Avoid being judgmental when learners are sharing their ideas, as this will close down debate and minimise the development of new ideas and understanding. The uncertainty created by the Concept Cartoons is productive.

The main body of a lesson should provide an opportunity for learners to explore, challenge or consolidate the ideas raised through the Concept Cartoon(s). Allow time at the end of the lesson for learners to share their ideas and opinions. Have they changed their minds and why? Do they want to add any new ideas to the Concept Cartoon?

Learners can create their own Concept Cartoons as a way of assessing and reviewing their current understanding.

If you want to know more about Concept Cartoons, and how they are used, please visit:

www.millgatehouse.co.uk

The Concept Cartoons in this book are also available on an interactive CD ROM. More about using the CD ROM is available on the following page.

Using Concept Cartoons

Science Concept Cartoons Set 2 CD ROM (available separately)

The CD ROM contains all the Concept Cartoons plus suggestions for follow up activities and background information together with extension ideas.

The speech bubbles on the CD ROM are fully writable.

Remember to print out any new Concept Cartoons that you create.

Using the features on the CD ROM

The writable speech bubble allows you to:
- change what the characters are saying
- add learners' ideas to those in the Concept Cartoon
- keep a printed record of learners' ideas
- create new Concept Cartoons
- encourage learners to create their own Concept Cartoons for other groups.

The follow up activities allow you to:
- share ways of exploring ideas with learners
- provide more challenges related to the concept being explored
- encourage some learners to work independently.

The background ideas enable you to:
- encourage learners to think about why the characters hold the alternative ideas
- share ways of exploring ideas with learners to find out more
- provide more challenges related to the concept being explored
- encourage some learners to work independently.

Any Concept Cartoons created by using this software are for use by the purchasing organisation **only and must not be given, or sold, to other individuals or organisations without prior permission from Millgate House Education.**

iii. Background Information

What are Concept Cartoons?

'Concept Cartoons are cartoon-style
drawings that put forward a
range of viewpoints about the
science involved in everyday situations.'

They are designed to intrigue, to provoke discussion and to stimulate thinking. By offering different ways of looking at a situation, Concept Cartoons make concepts problematic and provide a stimulus for developing ideas further. They do not always have a single right answer. The outcome may depend on circumstances, definitions and contextual factors. We believe that Concept Cartoons are a unique approach to teaching, learning and assessment in science.

Research into Concept Cartoons (Keogh and Naylor, 1999) identifies a number of features that help to make Concept Cartoons effective. These include:

· visual representation of ideas

· minimal text, in dialogue form

· using familiar situations

· offering alternative viewpoints, including the correct or most acceptable idea(s)

· common areas of misunderstanding, drawn from research and professional practice

· giving the alternatives equal status.

9

How are Concept Cartoons used?

Concept Cartoons are used in a variety of ways and in a wide range of settings. The most common reasons for using them are:

· making the learners' ideas explicit
· challenging and developing the learners' ideas
· illustrating alternative viewpoints
· providing a stimulus for discussion and argument
· promoting thinking and reasoning
· helping learners to ask their own questions
· creating a sense of purpose for the rest of the lesson
· promoting involvement and enhancing motivation
· posing open-ended problems
· as extension or consolidation activities
· as a summary of a topic or revision
· outside lesson time (e.g. homework).

Introduction

> 'Concept Cartoons are often used at the start of a lesson
> or topic as a stimulus for discussion, to identify areas of
> uncertainty and questions to be answered.'

Concept Cartoons are generally used to start a lesson or topic, but they can be used part-way through, or at the end, where the emphasis is on consolidating learning in a new situation. A short period of individual reflection on a Concept Cartoon before discussion starts can be useful for clarifying ideas; similarly some individual follow up after discussion and/or research can be useful for consolidating learning.

> 'Teachers and student teachers can also use Concept Cartoons
> for developing their own subject knowledge, by asking questions
> that they may not have thought of asking themselves.'

Research shows that many of the misconceptions held by children are retained into adulthood if they are left unchallenged. So as well as identifying the misconceptions and uncertainties that learners may have, teachers can use Concept Cartoons as a mechanism to review their own understanding, identify their own uncertainties, and ensure that they can justify which alternatives are correct.

'In each Concept Cartoon on the CD ROM, all the speech bubbles
are writable, to enable teachers and learners to create
their own Concept Cartoons.
The blank speech bubble allows learners to add their own ideas.'

The writable bubbles allow learners to add ideas and to include the mistakes that they think other people might make. Learners can create their own Concept Cartoons to illustrate possible areas of confusion or disagreement in a topic. Teachers can create their own Concept Cartoons to change the level of demand, or explore new concepts in the same situation.

Concept Cartoons and talk

Several features of Concept Cartoons help to promote talk between learners:
· The visual stimulus that, for many learners, is more engaging than a written or verbal stimulus
· The limited amount of text, which makes them especially suitable for learners with poor literacy (reading) skills
· The cartoon-style format and everyday setting give a strong message of familiarity, making the situations seem accessible
· Presenting ideas in deceptively simple situations promotes engagement with those ideas
· The dialogue between the characters seems to draw learners into their conversation, almost as though the learners are participating in their debate.

Although Concept Cartoons can be used individually, the interaction
between learners is important.

The value of encouraging learners to talk and argue about their ideas is widely recognised in schools. Teachers may have some concerns about managing this interaction, but using Concept Cartoons enables talk and argument to take place in a controlled and purposeful way. Concept Cartoons provide a focus, context and purpose for discussion, and they legitimise argument between learners. This kind of talk supports learning (Alexander, 2006). Having to justify one's ideas to other learners in the group is a powerful mechanism for developing deeper understanding.

11

> Using Concept Cartoons helps learners who lack confidence
> to share their ideas.

Having different characters putting forward the various alternatives and opinions helps to raise the status of each of the alternatives. The threat to a learner's self-esteem from putting forward incorrect ideas is therefore reduced. Having voices speaking for them helps to engage learners who may be reluctant to put forward their own ideas in case they are wrong.

Concept Cartoons and Learning

> 'The potential for generating cognitive conflict means that
> Concept Cartoons can be useful for all learners of science,
> regardless of their skills and experience.'

All of the alternatives in each of the Concept Cartoons are of equal status. There are no contextual clues, such as facial expressions or one character always having the best understanding, so all learners are likely to experience cognitive conflict and find that their ideas are challenged. Engagement with a Concept Cartoon can lead to a clarification of ideas, more secure learning and translation of knowledge into deeper understanding. One useful approach is to invite learners to work out why each of the characters might think their idea is correct.

Using Concept Cartoons has implications for the role of teachers and learners in the classroom. In many classrooms, learners put forward ideas and the teacher evaluates them. However with Concept Cartoons, alternative ideas are presented to the learners and they adjudicate between the ideas themselves. This is a fairly fundamental shift in role.

> 'Even though the teacher has the overall responsibility for managing
> learning, Concept Cartoons give learners more responsibility
> in the process and the value of their active involvement is enhanced.'

One very significant aspect of Concept Cartoons is motivation. As teachers we know that motivated learners are more effective learners, and that if learners are disaffected or alienated then there is often little real learning taking place. In our experience, teachers using Concept Cartoons consistently find that their learners are more motivated and engaged.

12

Concept Cartoons, Assessment and Learning

> 'Concept Cartoons help to put the principles of
> assessment for learning into practice.'

Concept Cartoons can be used for individual summative assessment. However they are probably more valuable as an assessment for learning tool, in which assessment is used to make learning more effective (Black and Wiliam, 1998; Black et al, 2002; Black and Harrison, 2004., Wiliam, 2011). As learners make their ideas public, the teacher is able to make informal judgements about their ideas, and the reasons behind them. It quickly becomes apparent whether learners have a good grasp of the concepts involved, are struggling to make sense of the situation or have firmly-held ideas that are influencing their thinking. The teacher can then take these ideas into account as the lesson progresses.

Meanwhile learners have the opportunity to discuss their ideas and to become more aware of what they and their peers think. Concept Cartoons encourage vigorous discussion and debate, and sometimes this can be enough to change a learner's idea or broaden their understanding. More frequently, the discussion raises the need for further exploration or research and begins the process of developing the learner's ideas. In this way using Concept Cartoons for assessment provides a starting point for learning and helps learners create their own learning agenda.

> 'Concept Cartoons identify what learners understand, and create the need
> for further enquiry and learning to resolve the conflict between ideas.'

The strength of this connection between assessment and learning was brought home to us when a teacher phoned late one evening to discuss a problem that she had:

" I've been using Concept Cartoons for assessment but I seem to be doing something wrong. When I use the Concept Cartoons I can't stop the children learning. What should I do? "

We have used the term 'Active Assessment' to describe this connection, in which purposeful, thought-provoking assessment activities become an integral part of the learning process (Naylor, Keogh and Goldsworthy, 2004). Concept Cartoons are not the only active learning approach to assessment. White and Gunstone (1992) also provide excellent descriptions of a range of techniques that can be used in a similar way. However Concept Cartoons are particularly effective at getting learners thinking about their own ideas and how they might need to develop or broaden. They promote metacognition – in other words they help learners to think about their own learning. Even quite young children have commented on how Concept Cartoons make them think about their own ideas and those of other people.

13

'The realisation that there can be lots of ways of thinking about a situation can be a powerful incentive to taking other people's ideas seriously.'

Getting learners to create Concept Cartoons for their peers or for younger learners is a good way of assessing their current understanding. They will need to think of possible alternatives as well as ensuring that they have included the acceptable scientific thinking.

Concept Cartoons and age range

When Concept Cartoons were first generated, we thought they would need to be targeted at particular ages. Experience has shown that this is not necessarily true, and that many of the Concept Cartoons can be suitable for a very wide age range.

Learners can often tackle a Concept Cartoon at their own level of understanding or experience, and will interpret the problems raised in different ways according to their own individual starting points.

The same Concept Cartoon may be used on more than one occasion and still provide a suitable level of challenge. The blank speech bubbles on the CD ROM add to the scope of many of the Concept Cartoons.

Life processes in animals and plants

1.1 What does alive mean?

1.2 Cells and atoms

1.3 When is it a baby?

1.4 Size of dividing cells

1.5 How does an embryo get bigger?

1.6 Fungi feeding

1.7 Germination: does size matter?

1.8 How do plants make food?

1.9 How do trees make wood?

1.10 Are plants sensitive?

1.11 Pollinate, fertilise or germinate?

1.12 Do plants move?

1.13 Do plants respire?

1.14 Do plants excrete?

1.15 Breathing or respiring?

1.16 Are bones alive?

1.17 High energy drinks

1.18 What is a balanced diet?

1.19 Why do we digest food?

1.20 Muscles and movement

1

15

I

Life processes in animals and plants

1.1 What does alive mean?

Put some cress seeds on a piece of moist paper towel and leave them for a few days. Talk about the changes you notice and what this tells you about whether the seeds are alive. Find three different definitions of life on the internet and discuss which you think is the most useful definition. How does a fire fit with these definitions?

Most plants reproduce by seeds. Seeds are plant embryos packed into a hard seed case, waiting to germinate, and they are alive. They can be almost too small to see or as big as a football. They need suitable conditions to germinate and start growing, including the temperature and amount of water. Fire isn't alive, it is a chemical reaction that releases energy by combining fuel with oxygen. It seems to do many of the things that livings things do, such as feed, grow, reproduce and excrete, but it is not made of cells. Modern biologists think that living things are able to control their internal environment, are organised into cells, and can change and evolve over time. Although there is no simple definition of life, a fire is not alive. Humans have been to the Moon and back, and at some point will probably go to Mars. What advice would you give to astronauts on Mars about how to decide whether something they find there is alive?

1.2 Cells and atoms

Use a microscope to look at some plant cells. The thin papery pieces in between the layers of an onion are good for this. Discuss what you know about plant cells and what they do. Look at the magnification on the microscope and try to estimate how big the plant cells are. Can you find out who first discovered cells using a microscope?

Living things are made of cells. There are different sorts of cell, each with its own function. Cells are like small building blocks that fit together to form tissues. Several different tissues form organs, like the heart or eye in an animal. Leaves, stems and roots are the organs in plants. Cells have many parts to them but they are mainly made from proteins, lipids (fats and oils), carbohydrates and water. Proteins, lipids and carbohydrates are complex molecules, made by living things from atoms of simpler substances like carbon, nitrogen, hydrogen and oxygen. It takes thousands of atoms to make even the simplest protein, and thousands of protein molecules to make a cell. Cells are very much bigger than atoms. You can see cells with a microscope but not atoms. Create a scale from 1 metre, 0.1 metre, 0.01 metre and so on down to 0.000000001 metre. Use your scale to show where atoms, cells and other tiny objects fit.

Life processes in animals and plants

1.3 When is it a baby?

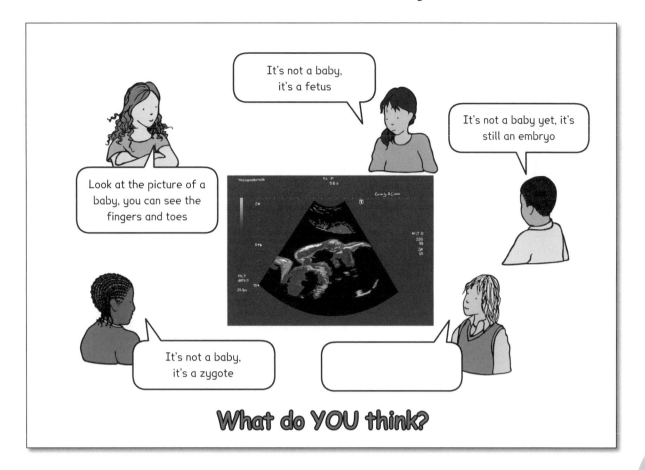

What do YOU think?

Find a series of images of babies developing inside their mother's womb in books or on the internet. Identify the stage at which you can tell it is a developing animal, and the stage at which you can tell it's a developing human. Find definitions for words like fetus, zygote and embryo, and see how they fit with the set of images. Why do you think that the developing baby's head is so big?

The process by which a baby forms has a number of stages. Fertilisation happens when the male sperm joins with the female ovum (egg cell) inside the female reproductive system. The sperm and ovum are called gametes. After fertilisation the fertilised ovum is called a zygote. About 12 hours after fertilisation the zygote starts to divide to produce new cells. A few days later the ball of cells is the size of a pinhead and it attaches itself to the wall of the uterus (a process called implantation), and the placenta and umbilical cord start to develop. The ball of cells is called an embryo until several weeks after fertilisation, when all of the major body organs are starting to develop. Then it is known as a fetus until the time of the birth. However, people often start to refer to it as a baby earlier than this. Draw a timeline to explain to someone else the different stages of development of a baby.

1.4 Size of dividing cells

Talk about what you mean when you say that a living thing grows and whether 'grow' can have more than one meaning. Discuss what might happen to the cells when a living thing grows. Draw some sketches of cells to show what you think is happening. Use a textbook or the internet to find out more about growth and cell division. Do you think cell division should be called cell multiplication?

Organisms can grow by increasing the number or the size of cells, or both. In animals, growth is mostly by increasing the number of cells, while in most plants the number and the size of cells increases as the plant grows. The number of cells increases by cell division, where one cell divides into two new cells. Cell division is part of a cycle, where cells grow until they reach a certain size, then they divide. The new cells then grow, and when they get big enough they can divide too. Complicated control factors stop cells dividing for ever. A cancerous tumour can form where the control factors don't work properly. Cell division is always needed to replace cells that get damaged or worn out, even when the organism doesn't get bigger. For example, in an adult the skin cells and red blood cells are constantly being replaced. Do you think cells divide at the same rate in a child and an adult? Sketch a graph to show how you think the rate of cell division changes during a human lifetime.

Life processes in animals and plants

1.5 How does an embryo get bigger?

Talk about what you think happens to the cells of an embryo when it grows. Draw some sketches to illustrate the different possibilities and talk about which of these seems most likely. Find out how many cells a typical human adult has and talk about where these came from. What happens when cells start to divide in a way that is out of control?

Growth in humans is quickest in the early stages of life. A single cell grows and then divides to make two identical cells. Each of these cells does the same thing to make four cells. This process carries on in an embryo to make 8 cells, 16 cells, 32 cells and so on. The increasing number of cells makes the embryo bigger. The cells stay about the same size as the embryo grows. When a baby is born the cells continue to divide as the baby grows. An adult is thought to have about 100 trillion cells. Most of our cells don't live as long as we do. Cells die and have to be replaced. In adults the rate at which new cells are made slows down so that it just replaces the cells that have died. Some specialised cells, like nerve cells, can be very long. However, the need to get oxygen and nutrients into the cell puts a limit on the size of most cells. Make a table to show which type of adult human cells are most likely to carry on dividing, and why.

1.6 Fungi feeding

Talk about the examples of fungi that you know. List the types of places where you would expect to see them. What does this suggest about how fungi might feed? Use a textbook or the internet to find out more about how fungi feed. Some fungi produce antibiotics, such as penicillin, that prevent other living things from growing. How do you think this can be helpful to a fungus?

Fungi are not plants or animals. The fungi include micro-organisms like yeasts and moulds, as well as larger ones like mushrooms, and they are classified in their own kingdom. Although structurally they can look like plants, they feed very differently. Fungi do not photosynthesise, so they can't make their own food. They have to get nutrients from a food source like we do. Most fungi live on dead and decaying materials and they are an important part of the decay process. They release enzymes to digest dead material and then absorb nutrients through threads called hyphae. Some fungi are parasitic and feed on other living organisms, including some that cause disease in humans. Some fungi have a symbiotic relationship with another organism, such as algae, helping to absorb water and minerals for the alga while the alga provides the fungus with nutrients. Fungi also help plant roots to absorb minerals from the soil and receive nutrients in return. Sketch an annotated diagram of a compost heap to show why fungi are important here.

Life processes in animals and plants

1.7 Germination: does size matter?

Collect a variety of seeds and put them in order of size. Sow several of each type of seed and measure the time it takes for germination to occur. Calculate the average time for each type. A scatter graph will be a good way to present the data and look for a relationship between seed size and germination rate. Do you think it will be an advantage for seeds to germinate quickly or slowly? Why?

Lots of things affect germination. Important factors are the amount of water, the amount of oxygen and the temperature. All of these affect enzyme activity and metabolism that are necessary for the seed to germinate. The thickness of the seed coat is important, because water has to pass through it to activate enzymes and start the germination process. For example, coconuts can take many months to germinate. Some seeds need special conditions to help them germinate, such as exposure to fire, soaking in water for a long time, or the right amount of light and darkness. The size of the seed does not affect the time taken to germinate. Some small seeds can start to germinate in less than a day, while others can take months. Seeds stay dormant until the conditions are right for them to grow, even if this takes many years. Scientists have managed to germinate seeds that are over a thousand years old. Use the information on seed packets to produce a table showing the conditions needed for germination of some common plants.

1.8 How do plants make food?

Talk about what you think is the best way to keep a potted plant healthy. Set up some investigations to find out whether plants can grow without soil, without water, without oxygen and without light. Look up the word photosynthesis and talk about what it means. Find out about root hairs, and use a microscope to look for these on the root of a germinating seedling. If plants don't take in food from the soil, why do you think they need roots and root hairs?

Green plants make their own food in a process called photosynthesis. The green chlorophyll in the cells of their leaves uses energy from sunlight to combine carbon dioxide and water in a chemical reaction to make glucose. Oxygen is released as a waste product during the process. The word 'photosynthesis' comes from the Greek for 'light' (photo) and 'putting together' (synthesis). Plants use the glucose in respiration to provide their cells with energy, just like animals do. Any spare glucose is turned into starch that the plant can store. Plants also need other essential nutrients (chemicals) that they can't make themselves, such as nitrogen, phosphorus and potassium. Plants need these to grow well and remain healthy. They absorb these nutrients, dissolved in water, through their roots, but they do not take in food through their roots. Create a table to show the similarities and differences between respiration and photosynthesis.

Life processes in animals and plants

1.9 How do trees make wood?

Think about what things a plant needs to grow successfully. Talk about whether seedlings can grow into healthy plants without soil. Plant some rapid life cycle seeds to see if they can complete their entire life cycle successfully without soil. Find out what fertilisers do in the life cycle of a plant. Why do you think fertilisers are often called plant food?

Plants grow because their cells divide to make new cells. The new cells form all the tissues and organs of the plant, such as roots, stems, leaves, flowers and seeds. Cells in the stems of some plants can develop into wood. For cells to divide they need a supply of energy and the raw materials to make new cells. Minerals from the soil don't provide the energy and only provide a very tiny amount of the material cells are made from. Plants make their own food by photosynthesis, where the green chlorophyll in the leaves uses energy from sunlight to combine carbon dioxide and water molecules in a chemical reaction. This reaction makes glucose and oxygen. The glucose can be used by the plant for energy, turned into cellulose or stored as starch. Plants use cellulose to create new cell walls and get bigger. In trees cellulose is the main material in the tissues that develop into wood. Wood strengthens the stems of trees so they can grow very tall. Imagine that you are producing an illustrated dictionary. Create an entry for the page in the dictionary that shows where wood comes from.

1.10 Are plants sensitive?

Think about how plants know which way to grow. Talk about how you think seeds manage to grow in the right direction to emerge from the soil. Germinate some seeds and see if the shoots all grow upwards. Put some germinating seedlings at an angle and see what happens to the shoots. What do you think happens to seeds germinated in a space rocket where the effects of gravity appear to be zero?

Living things are sensitive to their surroundings. This is one way we recognise that something is alive. Plants don't have a nervous system. Instead they use hormones called auxins that act as chemical messengers. These auxins enable the plant to sense some aspects of their environment, such as which way is up and which direction light is coming from. Auxins control lots of internal plant processes, such as making cells multiply and expand, controlling the development of fruits and controlling leaf fall. In cells close to the tip of a shoot, auxins make the lower layers of cells behind the tip multiply and expand, and this pushes the tip upwards against gravity. Auxins collect on the dark side of the shoot and makes the cells on that side multiply and expand, pushing the tip of the shoot towards the light. Find out about Charles Darwin's experiments on plant auxins, and produce a poster to illustrate what he learnt and how important his discoveries were.

26

1.11 Pollinate, fertilise or germinate?

Carefully dissect a flower and look at the different parts. See which parts you can identify. Simple flowers like tulips or daffodils are easiest to explore. Use the internet or a book to find out what the function of each part is. Watch insects visiting flowers, or find a video clip on the internet, to help you work out what happens when insects visit flowers. How do you think that pollen is transferred in flowers like grasses that don't attract insects?

Many flowers make sweet nectar to attract insects. As the insects push their way into the flower to collect the nectar, they accidentally pick up pollen on their bodies and transfer it to other flowers they visit. Bees also deliberately collect pollen to eat because it is full of protein. Pollen grains contain male sex cells that need to be transferred from one plant to another. Pollination usually means the transfer of pollen from the male parts of a flower to the female part (stigma) of another flower. The pollen grain grows a tube down towards the ovule inside the ovary of the flower, so that the male sex cells can travel down the tube and fertilise the ovule. The fertilised ovules then develop into seeds, and sometimes a fruit develops around the seeds as well. Draw an annotated storyboard sequence that illustrates how seeds develop from flowers and explains the differences between pollination, fertilisation, dispersal and germination.

Life processes in animals and plants

1.12 Do plants move?

Find some flowers growing near to you. Look at several different types of flowers. Photograph them in the morning and again in the evening. Compare the way the flowers and leaves face at different times of day. Research using the internet to see if you can find any video clips of plants moving. Why do you think that plants don't have legs to help them move like most animals do?

Plants don't have muscles. However many plants do have parts that move. One example is heliotropism, where plants move to keep their leaves or flowers facing the Sun. This is a slow movement, using special cells that take in or release water so that they expand or contract. As cells expand in one place and contract in other places, the leaf or flower moves. The Venus Flytrap is an example of a plant that moves quickly enough for us to see it as it catches insects to get extra nutrients. You can see video clips of this on the internet. Trigger hairs sense the movement of an insect, but scientists still don't fully understand how these plants move so quickly. Plants also look like they move as they grow. Climbing plants often spiral upward, coiling round their support, and grow so quickly that if you video them and playback the video quickly it looks like they are moving. Make a table to show what you think are the important similarities and differences between animal and plant movement.

Life processes in animals and plants

1.13 Do plants respire?

Think about where plants get their food from and what this food is used for. Talk about why plants need food if they get energy from sunlight. Discuss what gases are used and produced in photosynthesis and respiration, and what gas exchange you would expect from a plant at different times of day. How would you expect plant growth to affect carbon dioxide levels in the atmosphere?

Plants make sugars when they photosynthesise. Photosynthesis uses carbon dioxide, water and energy from sunlight, and oxygen is a waste product. Plant cells also respire, using the sugars they make and oxygen from the air to provide energy that they can use, just like animal cells do. During the day, plants photosynthesise and respire, so they use and produce oxygen and carbon dioxide at the same time. Generally in the daytime photosynthesis is much faster than respiration, so overall plants use carbon dioxide and produce oxygen. At night they can't photosynthesise because there is no sunlight, so they only respire and produce carbon dioxide. The cells in plants have a lot of carbon in them, especially woody plants. This carbon comes from the sugars they make in photosynthesis. Carbon dioxide is released as plants respire, when they die and decompose, or when they are burnt. Create a flow chart to show how plants and carbon interact. Include burning trees and coal in your flowchart.

1.14 Do plants excrete?

Talk about all the different substances (solid, liquid or gas) that come out of your body. Which of these do you think are waste? If these substances are waste, where do they come from and what processes produce them? Talk about whether other animals appear to produce similar kinds of waste and whether plants might also produce some of these wastes. What happens to our solid and liquid waste after we have been to the toilet?

Excretion is the word scientists use to describe the ways in which living things get rid of waste. Living things produce waste as part of their life processes. The main sources of waste in animals are digestion of food and cellular respiration. Chemicals that could be harmful if they remain in the body are removed by urinating, sweating, defecating and breathing. Excretion includes breathing out carbon dioxide. Plants also produce waste, including oxygen when they photosynthesise and carbon dioxide when they respire. These gases leave the plant through stomata, the tiny pores in their leaves. Some plants collect waste in their leaves and lose it when they shed their leaves in the autumn. Resin and gum also contain waste from plants. Some plant wastes can be stored inside the plant in a form that does not harm them. Produce a poster to explain where and how humans get rid of waste from their bodies.

Life processes in animals and plants

1.15 Breathing or respiring?

Talk about what happens when you breathe and why you breathe. What happens to the air that you breathe in? Why do you need to breathe out? What happens if you stop breathing? Use the internet or a text book to check your answers. Check whether there is a difference between breathing and respiration. How can some living things (e.g. yeast) manage without oxygen?

Respiration is a word used in two different ways. In health and physiology, it means transport of oxygen from the outside to the cells, and transport of carbon dioxide in the opposite direction. We draw air into our lungs when the diaphragm is pulled tight and the ribs rise as the muscles between them contract. In the lungs, oxygen passes into the blood and is carried by red blood cells to the cells of the body. Carbon dioxide made by the cells is carried by blood back to the lungs, where it passes into the lungs and is breathed out. Breathing is only part of the process of respiration, not all of it. In biology respiration has a different meaning. It refers to cellular respiration, which is a chemical process in animal and plant cells. In most situations this means oxygen is combined with sugars to release energy. In this reaction carbon dioxide is made and needs to be removed. Removal of this waste carbon dioxide is also a form of excretion. Create a flow chart or annotated diagram to show the movement of gases into, out of and inside the body.

Life processes in animals and plants

1.16 Are bones alive?

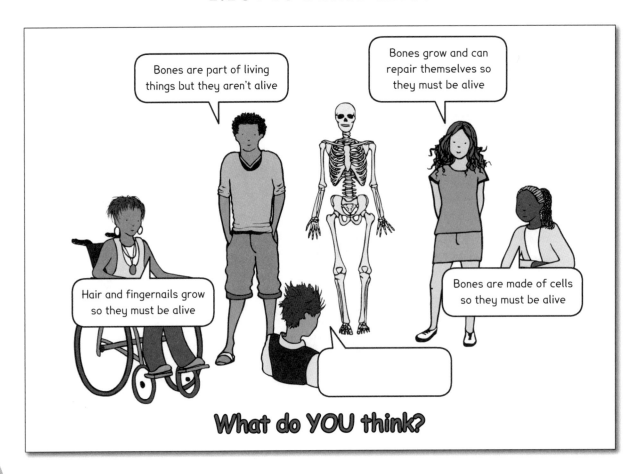

Talk about how you know whether or not something is alive. What evidence do you look for? Think of some things that are produced by animals or plants (such as a spider producing silk for its web, a cow producing milk, a tree producing resin or a crab producing a shell) and discuss whether these things are alive. What would you look for to decide? Viruses that cause diseases in animals and plants can reproduce. Are they alive?

When we judge whether something is alive we look for evidence of life processes. Living things move, respire, are sensitive, grow, reproduce, excrete and require nutrition. Cells within a living thing are alive, but only the organism as a whole displays all of the life processes. Not all of these processes go on in cells on their own. Bones are organs containing blood vessels, nerves and cells such as osteoblasts, so they are alive. The osteoblasts create new bone as a person grows or when bone is damaged and has to be repaired. The hard parts of bones are made from minerals such as calcium phosphate. Hair and fingernails are not alive. They are made of a protein called keratin and are not made of cells. Living cells in the skin produce the keratin that forms hair and nails, which is how hair and nails can grow. Create a list of things that are not alive and that are produced by living organisms.

Life processes in animals and plants

1.17 High energy drinks

Get hold of a high energy drink container and look at the ingredients. Discuss what each of the ingredients does, and use the internet to find out whether any of them have harmful effects. Work out how much of the body's daily energy needs are in one container. How many containers would you need for all the body's daily energy needs? What is likely to happen to someone who drinks a lot of high energy drinks but doesn't do a lot of exercise?

Sportspeople need enough energy to perform well. Our cells obtain energy by combining glucose with oxygen, and the faster our cells can do this, the more energy we have. Taking in extra glucose and breathing faster help our muscle cells to obtain energy faster. High energy drinks usually contain glucose, though not always. They almost always contain stimulants such as caffeine. Stimulants make the body act as though it has more energy. Glucose doesn't need to be digested so it can be used immediately. Starch and fat are good sources of energy too, but it takes longer for us to digest them. High energy drinks are fashionable, but they are not needed for a balanced diet. Taking high energy drinks without doing a lot of physical activity is likely to make people fat, and drinking large amounts can cause health problems because of the stimulants in the drinks. Create a two-colour poster to show the possible advantages and disadvantages of high energy drinks.

1.18 What is a balanced diet?

I have a balanced diet with equal amounts of different types of food

You shouldn't have fat or sugar in a balanced diet

A balanced diet is meant to make you lose weight

A balanced diet is what you need to stay healthy

What do YOU think?

Discuss what you think the difference is between a diet and a balanced diet. Find some examples of balanced diets on the internet. Identify what is included in a balanced diet and what (if anything) is excluded. Look at the side of a food package and check the information about what food groups it contains. What does it tell you about how much of each food group adults should eat? How would you expect a professional athlete's diet to be different from most people's diet?

Diet isn't just about losing weight. Diet means the range of food that someone normally eats. This can depend on factors like age, lifestyle, health needs, religion and personal preferences. There are six main food groups. A balanced diet provides the right amounts of each food group to stay healthy and maintain a stable body weight. We need different amounts of each of these food groups. For example, a small amount of salt is essential, but too much is damaging. Fat is essential in our diet too, but too much is not advisable. Sugar is a carbohydrate, and although it is not essential in our diet, small amounts of sugar aren't a problem. Athletes or other people who do a lot of physical exercise need a lot of carbohydrate in their diet. They normally get this through eating foods containing starch. We only need small amounts of vitamins and minerals in our diet. Get hold of some suggested diets and analyse whether or not they provide a balanced diet.

1.19 Why do we digest food?

Share what you know about the digestive system. Talk about how and why simpler organisms digest their food. Find out about how houseflies and fungi feed and how they use digestive enzymes, and discuss how this helps you to understand what goes on in the human digestive system. If our stomachs produce digestive enzymes, why do you think the stomach doesn't digest itself?

The human digestive system has two openings — the mouth and the anus. Anything that leaves through the anus isn't useful to us. The purpose of digestion is to break food down so that it is soluble and small enough to pass through the lining of the intestine into the bloodstream. Physical digestion begins when the food is cut into small pieces by our teeth. Chemical digestion happens inside the digestive system, starting in the mouth with saliva. Digestive enzymes break down food into the molecules it is made from. These molecules are small enough to pass through the cells lining the intestine and into the bloodstream. The blood transports digested food to all the cells in the body, where it is used to provide energy, for growth, repairing and replacing cells and other cell functions. Acid in the stomach also helps to destroy bacteria, though some toxins can't be broken down and can cause illness. Create a storyboard sequence to show what happens to an apple that you eat.

1.20 Muscles and movement

Hold on to the top of your arm and feel the muscles in it. Pull your arm up like a weightlifter, and feel the biceps getting fatter and shorter. Find a diagram of the muscles and bones in your arm and look for the biceps and triceps. Talk about what will have happened to your triceps when you pulled your arm up. Discuss what would have happened to your arm if you didn't have any bones in your arm. How many pairs of muscles can you find attached to bones? The meat in a butcher's shop is mostly muscle. Why do you think muscles are so red?

An animal's skeleton has three functions: supporting the body, protecting vital organs such as the brain, heart and lungs, and helping with movement. The joints in a skeleton allow an animal to move, but they do not cause it to move. This is the job of the muscles and bones. Muscles work by contracting and relaxing. When they contract they pull on the bones and make them move. Muscles can only pull on a bone; they cannot push the bone back into position. Because of this muscles almost always come in pairs, called antagonistic muscle pairs. One muscle contracts to pull the bone in one direction, while its paired muscle relaxes. To move the bone in the other direction the second muscle contracts while the first relaxes. Draw a sequence of diagrams to explain the action of the muscles as you move your arm up and down.

Life processes in animals and plants

Living things and their environment

2

2

Living things and their environment

2.1 How many senses?

Talk about what kinds of things you can sense. The five main senses are obvious, but there may be other things that you can sense as well. Talk about how you decide what counts as a sense and whether you would need more sense organs in order to have more senses. What about other animals? Can some animals sense things that humans can't? Make a list of animals with extra senses that humans don't have.

People have known about the traditional five senses of taste, smell, sight, hearing and touch for many years. However modern scientists recognise that there are more than five senses. The senses include receptors in the skin that sense heat and cold; the inner ear that senses position, movement and direction; the receptors in muscles and ligaments that sense where different parts of our body are (so you can touch your nose with your eyes shut); and receptors in different organs that sense pain. There are also lots of different receptors inside the body, to sense how much oxygen and carbon dioxide are in the blood, what the internal temperature of the body is, and when the bladder needs emptying. We tend not to notice these because the sense organs are not obvious like the eyes and ears. These 'extra' senses must be useful, otherwise they wouldn't have evolved in the way that they have. Choose one of these 'extra' senses and make a list of how being able to sense this is useful to us.

Living things and their environment

2.2 Big ears in elephants

Do some research using textbooks or the internet to find out about elephants' ears – what they look like, what their internal structure is, and what they are used for. Find pictures of all three species of elephant and talk about any differences between them. What other special adaptations do elephants have, and why are these adaptations important?

An elephant's ears help it to hear, but that isn't why they are so big. Their large flapping ears are very important to help them to control their body temperature. Because they are so large they are at risk of overheating in hot climates. Their ears are made from a very thin layer of skin with a rich blood supply. On hot days, elephants flap their ears to create a breeze. This flow of air cools the blood in their ears by as much as 6°C before it returns to the body. Elephants also use their ears to communicate. They challenge other elephants or predators by spreading their ears wider and making themselves look even bigger. They also use their ears during the mating period, when males fan their ears to help spread a scent that other elephants recognise. African and Asian elephants have different-sized ears. How might this be connected to where they live? Draw a diagram that will help someone to understand why elephants' ears are different sizes.

2.3 Big ears in rabbits

Do some research using textbooks or the internet to find out about rabbits' ears – what they look like, what their structure is, and what they are used for. Talk about why rabbits have their ears sticking up when they are grazing. Discuss what you would use your ears for if you were a rabbit. Rabbits communicate by stamping their feet or twitching their noses. Can you find out what these actions mean?

Rabbits don't sweat. Their ears are quite thin, with a lot of blood running through them, and this helps to cool the rabbit in hot weather. Rabbits also use their ears to communicate with each other. When relaxed their ears usually point backwards, but when feeling threatened their ears are more upright and other rabbits can see this. However, the main reason for the size of their ears is to protect them. Rabbits feed on low-growing plants, and they usually have their heads down as they graze. Rabbits are prey for several carnivores. When grazing their main protection is to hear their predators at a distance and run away, and their large ears give them sensitive hearing. Rabbits can move their ears one at a time to point in different directions, so this helps them to judge which direction a sound is coming from and escape from danger. Hares normally have even longer ears than rabbits, but the arctic hare has short ears. Draw a diagram to help someone understand why arctic hares' ears are different from most hares' ears.

2.4 How does a cactus feed?

Have a look at some cacti, or at pictures of cacti. Can you see any leaves? Can you see any spines? What is the stem like? What colour is the stem? Photosynthetic cells in leaves are usually green. Talk about which part of the cactus is most likely to photosynthesise. Cacti are adapted to live in hot dry climates in lots of ways. What can you find out about any of these adaptations? How would they help to protect cacti from hungry and thirsty animals?

In most plants photosynthesis occurs in the leaves. Cacti have become adapted so they can survive in hot, dry environments. In this environment normal leaves would lose too much water through transpiration and the cactus would die. In most species of cacti the leaves have evolved into spines that offer protection from grazing animals and provide some shade. The spines can't photosynthesise, but not having thin, flat leaves reduces the surface area and this reduces the loss of water. Because they don't have leaves that photosynthesise, cacti have developed enlarged stems with cells that can photosynthesise. The stem doesn't photosynthesise as efficiently as leaves do, so cacti are slow-growing. Think of some other ways that plants could be adapted to hot, dry environments and design a plant that could survive there.

2.5 What's in a food chain?

Food gives us energy, but where does the energy in our food come from? Think of some of your favourite foods and try to build food chains to show where the energy in your food comes from. Do all the food chains that you can think of begin with plants? Challenge your friends to find a food chain that doesn't start with a plant.

Food chains describe the transfer of energy through a habitat. Green plants use the energy in sunlight to make sugars by photosynthesis. They are called producers because they produce their own food. Algae are not plants but they also photosynthesise, so some food chains can start with algae as the producer, especially in the sea. Some bacteria can get energy directly from chemicals, so bacteria can also be the producer in a food chain. This can happen deep in the ocean where hot water, gases and other chemicals escape from the Earth's crust. Animals get their energy by consuming other organisms. Without plants, algae and bacteria there would be no energy available to animals because animals can't make their own food. All food chains finish with decomposers (fungi and bacteria) that break down dead organisms. Carnivorous plants are plants that can trap, kill and digest animal victims such as flies. These plants photosynthesise but also get nutrients from consuming animals. Create a food chain that includes a carnivorous plant. Who can create the longest food chain?

2.6 What do insecticides do?

Look at some greenfly on the shoots of young green plants. Estimate how many greenfly are on each shoot. Use the internet or a textbook to find out what greenfly eat, which animals eat greenfly and what food chains they are involved in. Talk about why gardeners might want to kill them. How do you think organic gardeners control greenfly if they don't use any insecticides?

Greenfly, whitefly and blackfly belong to a group of insects called aphids. They feed by sucking the nutrient-rich sap from plants. They can reproduce very quickly, producing hundreds of new aphids that can suck enough sap from a plant to damage or even kill it. Some insecticides kill aphids and nothing else, but many insecticides also kill useful insects. Aphids are small, succulent and slow-moving, so they make an ideal meal for lots of predators. If aphids have ingested any insecticide, the predators that feed on them will ingest it too. Each predator can eat a lot of aphids, so they will ingest a lot more insecticide and may be poisoned too. If the aphids are killed by the insecticide then the predatory insects may also starve, depending on what other food sources are available. Aphids can be controlled biologically by releasing predatory insects that eat the aphids. Gardeners can buy ladybird larvae to release in their gardens to eat aphids. Draw some food chains that include aphids, then predict what the different effects of insecticides and biological controls might be. Research using the internet to check whether your predictions are correct.

44

2.7 What happens when things die?

Have a close look at some soil to see what it is made from. Look for living things or anything that might have come from living things. Plan an investigation to find out what happens when fruit is left to rot. Talk to a gardener about compost heaps, what rots on a compost heap, whether everything rots and whether things completely disappear when they rot. What does compost have to do with growing plants?

Soil is a mixture of living and non-living materials. Part of soil is made from particles of broken-down rock. Another part is dead plants and animals in various stages of decay. When living organisms die they start to decompose and are eventually broken down into simpler forms of matter by bacteria and fungi. Some parts of dead organisms can take many years to rot, for example wood and bone. Earthworms and other invertebrates eat decaying plant material, which passes through them and adds nutrients to the soil. Nutrients are absorbed by plant roots, but plants do not use up the soil. Normally some decomposing plants and animals are added to the soil every year, so every year the soil level gets slightly higher. This is one of the reasons why we find objects from earlier times buried under layers of soil. Predict what you think will happen if decomposers are inactive (e.g. in boggy conditions), then use the internet to check whether your predictions are correct.

2.8 Bacteria in your body

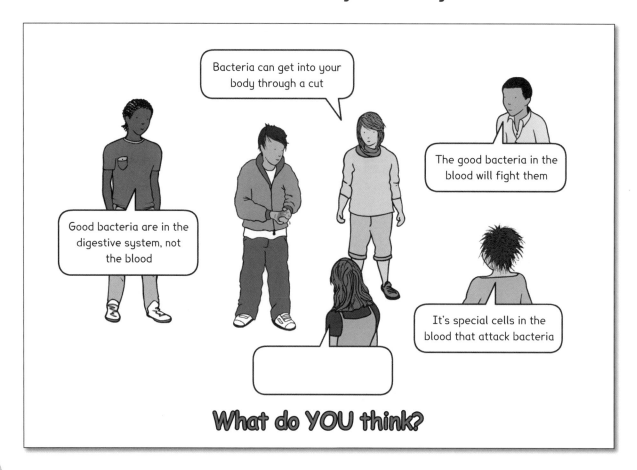

Most people think that bacteria harm us. Some people think that bacteria are only found in dirty places. Talk about whether you think these ideas are correct. Talk about what might happen if bacteria get into your body and how your body is adapted to stop bacteria getting in. Find out how your body protects itself from harmful bacteria if they do get in.

There are bacteria all around us. They live in soil, air, water and on the inside and outside of your body. Bacteria are not really 'good' or 'bad', they are just living things struggling to survive. Some bacteria are harmful to us, many bacteria are harmless, and some are actually helpful. Your digestive system has bacteria in it that help us digest our food, so these are useful bacteria. Some bacteria can cause illness, disease and even death. Your skin acts as a barrier to bacteria, but when you cut yourself they can enter your body and reproduce. They can produce chemicals (toxins) that make you ill. If bacteria get into your blood, white blood cells protect you by engulfing and digesting the bacteria or by making chemicals to destroy them. White blood cells are not bacteria. Chemotherapy is used to treat some cancers by stopping living cells from dividing. One side effect is that the body stops making white blood cells. Find out more about this, then produce a table to show the advantages and disadvantages of chemotherapy.

2.9 How do we get malaria?

Find out in which parts of the world malaria is common. Do these places have a warm or cool summer climate? Find out about mosquitoes, where they are found, how they feed and where they lay their eggs. People are advised to sleep under nets and use insect repellent to protect them from catching malaria. How do these precautions work?

Malaria is spread by female mosquitoes when they feed on human blood. When an infected mosquito bites you microbes called protists pass into your blood stream. The protists then cause malaria. Protists need both humans and mosquitoes to reproduce and their life cycle is quite complicated. The malaria protists can only be carried by mosquitoes that have fed on an infected person's blood. Some people think that you catch malaria from drinking dirty water, but this isn't true. Mosquitoes breed in still water, so warm places with large amounts of stagnant water will have more mosquitoes that are able to spread the disease. The name malaria comes from the Italian words for 'bad air', because people used to believe that air from decaying matter carries disease, but this isn't true either. Produce a short health guide for someone planning to move to a country where malaria is common.

2.10 What is a dragonfly?

Find a picture of a dragonfly in a book or on the internet. Look for distinctive features, such as how many body sections it has, how many legs, whether it has a skeleton, what its mouth parts are like, what type of eyes it has, how it reproduces and so on. Find out more about how animals are classified and where the dragonfly fits. Who first described the classification system that we use today? When did people begin to use this system?

All living things are placed into groups depending on their characteristics. The animal kingdom is divided into two large groups, vertebrates and invertebrates. Invertebrates are the group with no backbone. All the invertebrates can be divided into smaller and smaller groups, including classes and species. It's a bit like storing documents in folders inside other folders in a filing system. One of these groups is the insect group. A dragonfly is an insect as well as being an invertebrate and an animal, just like a document on a computer can be in a folder inside another folder. Insects are different from the other invertebrates. They are the largest class of organisms and account for over 75% of all animal species. Insects can be recognised easily because they normally have 6 legs, a body made of three parts, a pair of antennae and a pair of compound eyes. Find out more about insects, and create a poster to show why they are so important to humans.

Living things and their environment

2.11 Nothing growing under conifers

Find some pictures of pine forests on the internet. Look at how much vegetation is growing under the trees. Talk about why you see what you see in the pictures. Compare this with some pictures of deciduous woodland in summer and winter. What differences can you see? Talk about why there might be any differences. Plan an investigation to test at least one of your ideas.

There are lots of reasons plants don't grow under pine trees and other conifers. Pine trees are often planted very close together, so they block out most of the light and make it difficult for other plants to photosynthesise. This stops lots of plants from growing, though some plants that prefer shade might survive. Pine trees take up most of the available water that other plants need to grow. The pine trees also take nitrogen and other nutrients from the soil, which makes it harder for other plants to grow. The dead pine needles also create acidic conditions and remove nitrogen from the soil as they slowly decompose. Pine trees are often planted in places where other plants find it hard to survive, including very acidic soils and places that are cold and exposed. Fungi often grow very well under conifer trees. Can you explain why?

Living things and their environment

2.12 Do seedlings compete?

Sow some seeds or plant some seedlings in a tray. Give some plenty of space, and plant others very close together. Observe what happens as they grow. Talk about what you see and try to explain your results. When gardeners sow seeds in a tray they often sow far too many and then thin them out after they have germinated. Why do you think they do this?

Plants and animals in the same area will compete with each other for resources such as food and water. Getting hold of these resources can mean the difference between survival and death. Generally the most successful animals or plants survive to pass their genetic information on to the next generation. Plants compete with each other, regardless of species, as they all need a supply of water, energy from sunlight and nutrients from the soil. If you crowd a lot of seedlings into a tray they may be short of water because the small amount of compost in the tray can't hold much water. As they grow taller they may cast shadows on the other seedlings and stop them getting energy from sunlight. This could delay or stop their development into healthy mature plants. What advice would you give to a gardener who decides to get a bigger crop by sowing lettuce seeds much closer together than is indicated on the seed packet? Draw a diagram to show what the gardener needs to know.

2.13 How did giraffes evolve?

Use a textbook or the internet to find out about Lamarckism, named after the French scientist Lamarck. Also find out about Darwin and his views on evolution. Talk about how Lamarck and Darwin would each explain how the giraffe got its long neck. Which do you think is the more plausible explanation? Which do you think modern scientists agree with? Check your ideas on the internet.

Animals of the same species are never identical; there are always small differences between them. We call these differences variation. The variation is an accident, and sometimes it can give the animal an advantage that helps it survive better. If the animal passes this variation on to its offspring then they will have the advantage as well. When times are difficult (e.g. if there is little food or water), the animals with an advantage are likely to survive better and produce more offspring. Over millions of years this can lead to big changes in the species or to completely new species developing. The individual animals don't change; it's the population of animals that gradually changes over a long period of time. This process is called evolution. It is one of the most important ideas in biology. Use this idea to explain how polar bears and brown bears, or foxes and arctic foxes, have evolved to survive in their environments.

2.14 Streamlining in penguins

Make sure you know what the word 'streamlined' means. Check it if you are not sure. Look at a picture of a penguin and talk about how it is streamlined. Can you find more examples of when streamlining is found in nature? How does streamlining help? Can you find examples of how streamlining is used in industry?

Even though there is some uncertainty in the details of how lots of organisms evolved, all the evidence we have supports the main ideas in the theory of evolution. Lots of fossils have been found (dating as far back as 36 million years) that help us to understand how penguins evolved. It is believed that penguins evolved from a type of bird that could fly. However, their diet was mostly fish, so any mutations that enabled them to swim rather than just skim the water would have helped them to feed more successfully. This increased their chances of survival, so the mutations were more likely to be passed to future generations. Other mutations led to streamlining, which enabled penguins to swim more rapidly and catch more fish. These mutations would also be passed on to the penguins' offspring, and the penguins with the mutations would be more likely to survive and leave more offspring. Penguins evolved to be streamlined because the advantage helped them to survive. Create a poster that shows what the intermediate stages might have looked like between a modern penguin and a flying bird that feeds on fish.

2.15 Which animals evolve?

Talk about what the word 'evolution' means. Share your ideas about whether all animals have evolved over time, or whether some have never changed. Talk about whether you think an elephant has always had a trunk and whales have always had a thick layer of blubber. Look up drug-resistant bacteria and when they were first identified. What can you find out about how the theory of evolution developed?

Evidence gathered from fossils and the varieties of animals and plants alive today provides strong evidence for evolution. It is the only reasonable explanation of how living things have changed over time, enabling them to survive in different environments. All living things can evolve, but where something is already suited to its environment then it won't necessarily change any further. Some microorganisms have not changed for millions of years because they are successful. Other disease-causing microorganisms are evolving and becoming resistant to drugs. They are not getting bigger or more complex; they are still very simple, single-celled organisms. Their new, drug-resistant characteristics allow them to survive successfully without getting more complex. For many living things getting bigger would not be an advantage. Think of a very hot environment and design an organism that could live there. What features will it have? How might the specie evolve if the environment changes to become colder?

2.16 Drug-resistant microbes

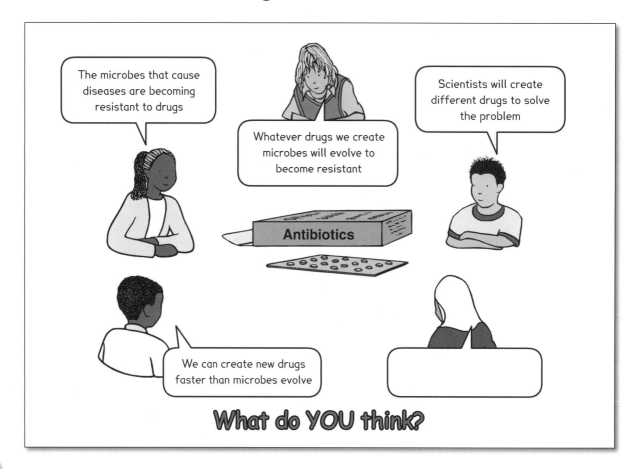

Discuss what you know about different groups of microorganisms that cause disease and what diseases they cause. Find out whether all diseases caused by microorganisms can be cured using drugs. Research some recent news reports about MRSA, what it is, where it is a problem and why. Imagine life without drugs to fight disease. Can you find out what life was like before antibiotics were discovered?

Antimicrobial drug resistance happens when a microorganism develops a mutation in its genes that causes it to become resistant to a drug designed to treat it. Microbes without the mutation are killed by the drug, but those with the mutation survive and reproduce. The mutation can lead to the whole population of microbes becoming resistant over a relatively short period of time. Some microorganisms carry several resistance genes to different drugs, and these are described as 'superbugs' or multidrug resistant (MDR). Scientists work to produce new drugs to treat the problems of drug-resistant microorganisms, but trialling new drugs takes many years. Microorganisms can mutate and evolve in just a few years. Whatever new drugs are created, microorganisms will evolve over time to become resistant. What advice would you give to a farmer who breeds pigs and plans to include antibiotics in their food to prevent them getting diseases? Work together to produce a short advisory leaflet for farmers.

Environmental issues

3

3

Environmental issues

3.1 Recycling or reusing?

Find out about recycling and reusing containers in your town. Which containers are recycled and which are reused? Talk about why it might be better to reuse some containers and recycle others. Invite somebody in from a local organisation that recycles things. Find out more about recycling and reusing materials in different countries from books or the internet. Look at recycling and reuse case studies on websites such as Practical Action. What happens to things that can't be recycled or reused?

Enormous amounts of packaging and containers are wasted each year. Reusing and recycling reduce the amount of resources we use, the amount of energy we need, and the amount of waste that we produce. For example, glass is made mostly from sand, but it takes a lot of energy to turn sand into glass. Glass is recycled by melting and reforming it into new glass containers, and this needs less energy than making new glass. We can wash and reuse glass containers at home, or old glass containers can be collected, transported and sterilised so they are safe to use. Reusing glass means no energy is needed to melt it, and this needs less energy than recycling glass or making new glass. What other containers can be safely reused? Think about how you can recycle and reuse things at home and create a poster or presentation of your ideas.

3.2 What do we do with nappies?

Look at all the different materials that are used to make a new disposable nappy (or diaper). You could take an unused one apart. Make a table to compare reusable and disposable nappies. Find out about raw materials used, energy consumption, water consumption and waste disposal. Find out how hot the water has to be to get them clean. What type of nappy did you have when you were a baby? Talk to other people who use nappies. Which type do they use and why? How much do they think about the environment?

Nappies (or diapers in the USA) are an important aspect of growing up. One baby may have as many as 6 000 nappy changes. Disposable nappies are convenient and easy to use, but they use lots of resources and create lots of waste. Disposable nappies are buried in landfill sites where they take many years to decompose. Landfill sites use valuable land and cause environmental problems. Reusable nappies need to be washed to get them clean and then dried. This takes effort from us and needs energy. Overall reusable nappies generally need more energy than disposable ones. However washing them at 60°C is hot enough to get them completely clean, and it may be possible to hang them on a line to dry them. This reduces the energy needed so in these circumstances reusable ones would be better than disposable ones. Produce a guidance leaflet for a new parent deciding which type to use. Give it to some parents and see what they think.

Environmental issues

3.3 What's the best use for land?

Think of all the things land can be used for. Talk about your most recent journey, and list all the different things you saw land being used for. Compare several people's answers. What answer would you get in a different part of the country, or a different part of the world? Use the internet to find out if there is a shortage of land for housing, for farming animals, or for growing biofuels. Why is it important that some land isn't used by humans?

We use land for many different things, and it is important for other living things too. If the land is good enough to produce food, then growing crops is the most efficient way to feed people. If the land is poorer, then farming animals for meat and milk might be a better way to produce food. Producing biofuels can provide us with energy and reduce our use of fossil fuels. People need places to live so building houses is important, but when land is built on it is unlikely to be turned back into a more natural environment. Having a more natural habitat with animals and plants is also very important for the environment. Deciding what is most important may depend on where you live. Imagine there is a piece of land available locally. Split into groups and each group can take a different use for the land. Can you persuade others that yours is the most important?

3.4 Do we need an incinerator?

Get hold of some information about incinerators. Use more than one source to get a range of views. Make a table to show the advantages and disadvantages of incinerators. Split into groups for and against incinerators and use the table to help you present an argument to an opposing group. Are you able to convince them with your arguments?

Coal fires, wood-burning stoves, gas heaters, cars and incinerators all produce pollution. Incinerators are becoming more common because they get rid of rubbish and can generate electricity or heat homes at the same time. Some people don't like incinerators near where they live because of possible pollution. Modern incinerators have many different features to make sure that the gases they release are no more polluting than coal-fired power stations or wood-burning stoves. They also generate electricity so less coal, oil or gas has to be burnt. This reduces the total amount of carbon dioxide being made to generate electricity, because the carbon dioxide that is made as the rubbish burns would be released anyway as it decomposes. Incinerating rubbish can also produce hot water that can be used to heat local houses. Imagine that your town has to deal with all its own rubbish. Design a strategy to deal with it. What will happen to rubbish from your town if you decide not to incinerate any of it?

Environmental issues

3.5 Should we use electric cars?

Find some information about electric cars. Use more than one source to get a range of views. Make a table to show the advantages and disadvantages of electric cars compared to other cars. Talk about your table. What advice would you give to someone who wants to buy a car? Are there any other types of cars that don't have to be filled with fossil fuels to work?

Electric cars need electricity, and the electricity they need has to be generated somewhere. If the electricity is made using fossil fuels, then it produces pollution and greenhouse gases at the power station. Generating electricity and sending it through wires to towns and cities is not very efficient. If the electricity is made using renewable sources of energy then this makes electric cars much better for the environment. All cars need energy and resources to build them, and this has an impact on the environment too. If electric cars are charged at night, when electricity demand is low, this can help by using spare electricity generating capacity, since turning power stations on and off is very inefficient. Electric cars do produce pollution and greenhouse gases, but less than other cars do. Imagine you have a lot of money to invest in local public transport. What forms of transport would you invest the money in, and why? Do others agree with you?

3.6 Is nuclear energy green?

What do you think people mean when they talk about green energy? Get hold of some information about nuclear energy. Use more than one source to get a range of views. Find out what nuclear reactors use as fuel. Is it a fuel in the same way that fossil fuels are? What kind of waste do they produce and what happens to the waste?

Nuclear reactors use radioactive substances to heat water, which is then used to generate electricity. Nuclear reactions release lots of energy without using much nuclear fuel. Nuclear fuels will last for thousands of years, but they have to be mined and processed and this requires energy. Nuclear power stations take a lot of energy and resources to build, and they are dangerously radioactive when they are too old to use anymore. They don't produce greenhouse gases like carbon dioxide, but they do produce radioactive waste that has to be processed carefully. Some of the waste needs to be stored for hundreds or even thousands of years before it is safe, and nuclear accidents can be very serious. Overall nuclear reactors are much more energy-efficient than coal, gas or oil. Make a table to show the advantages and disadvantages of nuclear energy compared to other possibilities. Imagine you are the Minister for energy policy. Use your table to write a brief policy statement about whether to invest in nuclear power stations in the future. Do others agree?

Environmental issues

3.7 Is energy free?

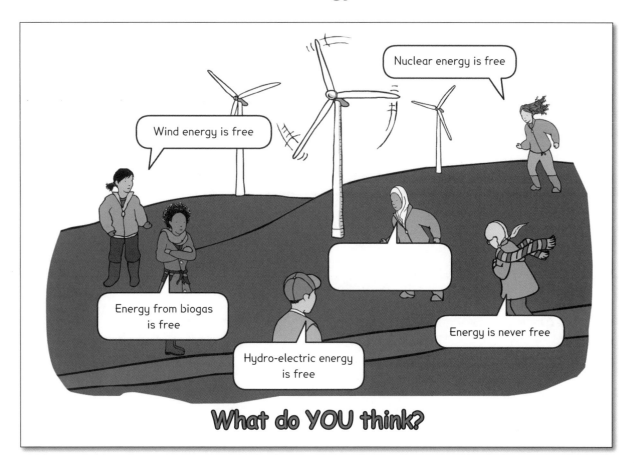

Talk about what you mean by free energy, and the difference between energy that is free and energy that isn't. Use the internet to research wind turbines, hydroelectric turbines, nuclear power stations and biogas. Find out where the energy comes from and what happens to it. How do these compare with other sources of energy? What do the terms renewable and non-renewable energy mean, and how are these connected to climate change?

Making energy available in a useful form always costs something, even if we use natural resources. Wind turbines are expensive to build, and need to be strong to resist the weather. Hydroelectric dams are expensive to build and need to be strong to hold back the water they use to make electricity. Biogas requires anaerobic digesters to break down waste. Even solar panels are expensive to install. All of these natural sources can provide energy, but there is a cost involved in creating and maintaining them. Nuclear power stations are very expensive to build to ensure that they are safe and don't leak radiation. Nuclear waste stays radioactive for thousands of years and needs to be stored carefully. In some remote rural areas, small scale renewable energy is the only option available. Produce a chart to show the advantages and disadvantages of different ways of producing electricity. Use websites such as Practical Action to find out more about how to select the best type of renewable energy.

3.8 Are biofuels useful?

Talk with your friends about what biofuels are. Use the internet to get more information about what biofuels are, where they come from, how they are used and any disadvantages of biofuels. Different sites give different information, so use more than one site to get a range of views. Find out about whether using biofuels saves energy, and if so, how much. How much do people use biofuels now? Why do some people say that growing biofuels puts up the price of food?

Biolfuels are made from plants or waste materials. They are alternatives to fossil fuels, so using biofuels can reduce the amount of fossil fuels we use. Biofuels release carbon dioxide when they burn, but they take up carbon dioxide as they grow. They produce some other pollution as well. Many of them are cleaner than fossil fuels but some produce as much pollution as oil or coal. Calculating the cost of biofuels is complicated. Biofuel crops may use fertiliser and chemicals, and the machines that harvest and process them need fuel. Overall the amount of fossil fuels that we save may be very small. Scientists are researching new biofuels that don't need much energy to produce them, don't create a lot of pollution and don't require much land to grow them. What can you find out about these? Choose one biofuel that you think we might be using in 20 years time and try to sell the idea to others. Are they convinced?

3.9 Is global warming happening?

Use a science dictionary to find out the difference between weather and climate. Use a science textbook or the internet to find out about global warming, why this is happening and what the effects of global warming might be. Use more than one source to get a range of views. How does global warming fit with the climate where you live? See if your parents or grandparents can help with this question, or use the internet to find weather records going back over many years.

Climate is different from weather. Weather describes what we experience day by day, such as temperature, rainfall, wind and other conditions. It can change a lot over just a few hours. The climate describes weather patterns over many years. For several decades the Earth's average temperature seems to be getting higher. Scientists think this is probably caused by increasing amounts of carbon dioxide in the atmosphere, which is increasing the greenhouse effect. This pattern is called global warming. Weather is caused by lots of different things and is hard to predict. Even though global warming may be happening we can still get very cold weather some of the time. Some places are predicted to get colder or wetter because of global warming. If global warming continues, what other effects might it cause and why? Create an interactive display of frequently asked questions about global warming and information to answer these questions.

3.10 Impact of climate change

Use a science textbook or the internet to find out about whether and how the climate is changing. Use more than one source to get a range of views. Look for evidence such as the impact on glaciers, rainfall, coral reefs, drought and distribution of plants and animals. Use the internet to find weather records over many years and find out about the climate where you live. What difference will it make to our lives if the climate is changing? Why do you think some people don't accept scientific evidence about climate change?

Climate is different from weather. Weather describes what we experience day by day, such as temperature, rainfall, wind, etc. The climate describes weather patterns over several decades. There is strong evidence that the Earth's climate is changing. Scientists think this is probably caused by increasing amounts of CO_2 in the atmosphere, which is increasing the Earth's average temperature. Because of this the climate is becoming more changeable, with more extreme weather events happening. Some places now get more rainfall than they used to. This can cause flooding so people lose their homes. Other places get less rainfall, causing drought so crops don't grow. If the climate is changing, what effects is it causing and why? Use websites such as Practical Action to create an interactive display of frequently asked questions about climate and information to answer these questions.

Environmental issues

3.11 The greenhouse effect

Use a textbook or the internet to find out about the greenhouse effect. Use more than one source to get a balance of views. Do different sources agree, or do different people have different opinions? Why might this be? Greenhouses are useful to us, so why do you think the greenhouse effect might be a problem?

Radiation from the Sun travels through space to the Earth. Some of it reflects back into space. The land, sea and atmosphere absorb some of the radiation, and they radiate infrared radiation, some of which travels out into space. 'Greenhouse gases' in the atmosphere absorb some of the infrared radiation and radiate it back towards the surface. This stops it escaping into space, so the Earth gets warmer. This is a natural process. Water vapour, CO_2 and methane are all greenhouse gases. Burning fossil fuels increases the amount of CO_2, and this increases the greenhouse effect. CO_2 makes the rain slightly acidic, but it's mainly NO_2 and SO_2 that react with water droplets in the atmosphere to make them more acidic. Ozone is a rare type of oxygen found high in the atmosphere. It absorbs damaging ultraviolet radiation, but does not cause the greenhouse effect. There is a 'hole' in the layer of ozone above the north and south poles, caused by gases such as CFCs (chlorofluorocarbons). Create an illustration to show the differences between the greenhouse effect and the hole in the ozone layer, and how they affect our lives.

3.12 Where should we grow tomatoes?

Find out about the growing season for tomatoes in this country. Make a table to show in which months they can be grown here. Find out where they come from in the other months. Where do the other fruits and vegetables that you eat come from? Use the Food Connections activity from Practical Action to help you work out what difference it makes if we grow foods locally or import them.

In many countries fruits and vegetables can only be grown outside at certain times of year. If we want them all year round they must be grown in greenhouses or imported from other countries. Heating greenhouses and transporting food requires energy. If the energy comes from fossil fuels this adds to the CO_2 going into the atmosphere. Greenhouses can be heated using renewable energy, but transport using renewable energy is more difficult. Eating foods that grow well in our climate minimises the energy needed to produce and transport it. It's complicated, because in some countries growing food for export is important for creating jobs. Recently large corporations have been buying land from small farmers in Africa and Asia, so those farmers lose their livelihood. You can find out more about threats to small farmers at websites such as Practical Action. Some foods are labelled as Fairtrade. What is the Fairtrade organisation and how can you, your school and your town support Fairtrade? Make a Fairtrade leaflet to share your ideas.

Environmental issues

3.13 Do we need to save water?

Find out about where your water comes from and how it is treated before it gets to you. Make a comparison table to show the differences between collecting water yourself, getting it from a well, or getting it from a tap. Does everyone in your class get water from the same place? How do you think you would manage if there is a water shortage?

Food, shelter and water are essential for survival. If you can always get clean water from a tap you might not think about where it comes from, but it has to be collected, stored, cleaned and transported to you. The water cycle supplies most places with some water as water evaporates from the sea, condenses as clouds and forms rain that falls on the land. In many parts of the world rainfall is not dependable. Countries that usually have plenty of rain can sometimes have a drought, and climate change is making rainfall more unpredictable. Even in very wet periods, water has to be collected and stored for when it is drier. Imagine that the climate becomes hotter and drier. Think about different people who need access to water, such as a farmer, a householder, a factory owner using water-cooled machinery, a garden centre manager, a golf club owner, etc. Share these roles out and put forward an argument for why the person you represent should get access to water. Try to create a strategy to reduce water use, based on your arguments.

3.14 The impact of deforestation

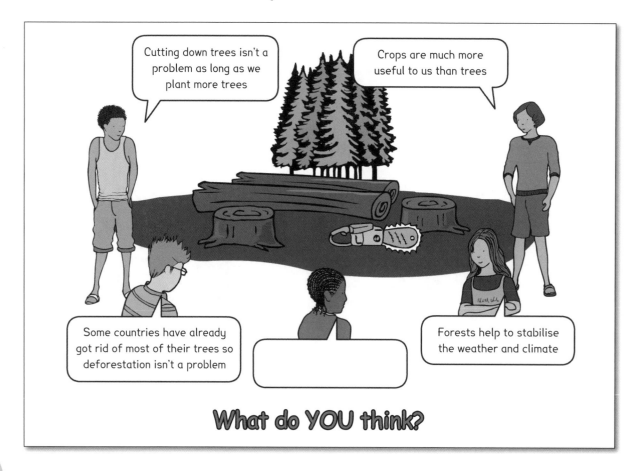

Use the internet to find information about the environmental impact of trees, including climate change. Look for websites of organisations such as the Forestry Commission that know a lot about trees and their environmental impact. Find out where deforestation is happening and what the impact is likely to be. If trees are useful, why do you think people cut them down?

We can eat crops but we can't eat trees (although some trees produce fruit). However trees are really useful in other ways. Plants remove CO_2 from the atmosphere as they photosynthesise and grow. Trees are large and live for a long time, so a lot of carbon is locked up in their cells. If a tree is cut down all the carbon in it returns to the atmosphere as it rots or is burnt for fuel. The carbon in trees that have turned into coal has been kept out of the atmosphere for millions of years. By comparison crop plants remove much smaller amounts of carbon, and it returns to the atmosphere more quickly. So trees are important for reducing climate change. They also help to stabilise temperatures, they are an important part of the water cycle, and they prevent soil erosion and flooding. Trees provide a rich habitat for other living things, especially old established trees that provide a wide variety of habitats and ecological niches. When they are removed the living things that depend on them also die. Create a compare and contrast table to compare the likely environmental impact of trees and crops.

70

Properties of materials

4

4

Properties of materials

4.1 Can we compress gases and liquids?

Squash a balloon and see what it feels like. See if there is any difference when the balloon is full of water. Push a plastic syringe with your finger over the hole at the end. What happens? See if there is any difference between a syringe filled with water or air. What happens if you squash a bag full of air very hard? Does the material the bag is made from make a difference? Why do you bounce upwards when you jump on a bouncy castle?

Filling a bag with air or water traps the particles so they cannot escape. When you squash the bag of air there is space between the air particles so they can move closer together. If you had the strength and the bag was strong enough, you could squash them into a space thousands of times smaller. The particles do not change size; it is only the space between them that changes. There is very little space between the particles in a liquid. They are packed together almost as densely as those in a solid, so it is hard to squash most liquids more than a tiny amount. The particles touch each other, but they are not fixed in position so they can flow around each other. This is why liquids are runny. The words pneumatics (gases) and hydraulics (liquids) are related to how materials behave when they are squashed. Create a guide to how, where and why pneumatics and hydraulics are used in everyday life.

4.2 How does liquid get into a syringe?

Pull the plunger back on a syringe so there is a little bit of air in it, and put your finger over the end. Pull the plunger back. What do you notice? Talk about what is happening to the air inside and how the pressure of the air inside the syringe will change. How does filling a pipette with water compare with filling a syringe?

Air is made up of a huge number of particles that move around and collide with every surface they are in contact with. These collisions push on those surfaces and cause air pressure. There is a lot of empty space between the air particles, so air can be squashed or spread out. As air is squashed the pressure goes up, and as air is spread out the pressure goes down. Pressure can only push on things, not pull on them. Air pressure pushes on the surface of liquids as well. When you pull the plunger back in a syringe, the air particles in the syringe are spread out more. The space that is created has a lower pressure compared to outside, so liquid is pushed into the syringe by the air pressure on the surface of the liquid. This continues until the pressures inside and outside the syringe are equal. If you push the plunger the pressure inside is bigger than outside and the liquid squirts out. Draw a diagram or make a model to show how we use air pressure to breathe in and out.

Properties of materials

4.3 What are clouds, mist and fog?

Talk about what happens to your breath when you breathe out on a cold day and why you think this happens. Watch smoke rise from a chimney or fire. Talk about whether smoke is likely to be made from solids, liquids or gases. Talk about what fog is like and how you can decide if fog is the same as smoke. What does the word smog sound like? What is it likely to be made from, and where is it likely to be found? Check your answers on the internet.

Clouds, mist and fog are all made from tiny droplets of liquid water that form when water vapour condenses. These droplets are so light that they don't fall down as rain. They are blown about by the wind. Smoke is a mixture of solids, liquids and gases that is made when something burns. It is a complicated mixture of chemicals, some of which are harmful if you breathe them in. Fuels burn more completely if there is a lot of oxygen present, and this makes less smoke. Smog is a type of pollution usually found in cities. It is caused by vehicle exhaust fumes and smoke from burning fuels like coal. Sunlight acts on these fumes and changes them chemically. Smog can build up to damaging levels when there is no wind to blow it away. Create a map showing which cities in the world suffer from bad smog and why this is.

Properties of materials

4.4 How cold are things in a fridge?

Put a temperature probe inside a container of water at room temperature and put this inside a fridge. Observe and talk about how the temperature inside the fridge changes. Try it with different containers, including plastic and metal. How many different ways can you think of to cool things and keep them cool without a fridge? What are the advantages and disadvantages for each method?

Keeping milk cool helps to keep it fresh. When you put something warm into a fridge it loses energy. The bigger the difference between the temperature of the fridge and the milk, the faster the milk loses energy. As the temperature of the milk gets closer to the temperature inside the fridge, the loss of energy from the milk slows down. It takes longer for the milk to cool by the last few degrees than the first few degrees. A big bottle of milk takes longer to cool down than a small one because it has more energy to lose. The milk can never get colder than the fridge. If you put frozen milk into a fridge it gains energy from the fridge, warms up and melts. Metals are good thermal conductors, so milk in a metal container loses energy quickly, but still reaches the same final temperature. Sketch a temperature change graph for when a container of water at room temperature is placed in a fridge, in a metal bowl or in a thermos flask.

Properties of materials

4.5 Does helium have a weight?

It is difficult to weigh gas in a floating balloon. You can find out whether air has mass and weighs something using balloons full of air. Put one on each end of a lever balance and carefully pierce one through a piece of tape stuck on the balloon. Observe what happens and talk about why. However you can't weigh helium like this. Research on the internet to find the weight of a helium cylinder when it is full and when it is empty. How will the weight of the helium gas cylinder change as it is used to fill balloons?

All gases have mass, and gravity pulls on them so they must have weight. If you put helium in a balloon then it must get heavier. So why does it float? If you push something that floats so it goes underwater, it pushes some water out of the way and the water pushes back. We call this force buoyancy, and it pushes the object back towards the surface. Air pushes on objects as well. Helium is a very light gas that is much less dense than air. A tiny mass of it takes up a lot of space. A balloon filled with helium gas does get heavier but it also becomes less dense than the air around it. The air pushes on the balloon and makes a buoyancy that is big enough to make the balloon float upwards. Create an annotated drawing to show why a helium-filled balloon floats in air and an air-filled balloon doesn't.

4.6 Different materials, different atoms?

Talk about what you think atoms are, and what the difference is between atoms and molecules. Use the internet, books and other sources to find pictures and information about them. Using atomic models might be helpful. Talk about what you think different materials such as copper, water and plastic are made from. Where do the words atom and molecule come from? How can we be sure that atoms exist if they are too small to see?

Everything is made from atoms. They make up the elements, such as oxygen, mercury and iron. There are three basic parts to an atom – electrons, protons and neutrons. All the atoms of an element are the same. However, the atoms of each element are different from the atoms of other elements because they have different numbers of electrons, protons and neutrons. The atoms in some elements can be arranged in different ways and form different materials. For example, carbon can be charcoal, graphite, diamond or graphene depending on the arrangement of its atoms. Atoms of different elements can combine to make molecules, such as hydrogen and oxygen which combine to make water molecules. Different combinations of atoms make different materials. Materials exist in different states, as solid, liquid or gas. The atoms in the solid, liquid and gas forms of any material are the same, but they are arranged differently. Draw an annotated diagram to show how you think nuclear reactors change one element into another.

Properties of materials

4.7 What is a pure substance?

Use an online dictionary to find out what element, compound and mixture mean. Talk about how this helps you to decide what 'pure' means. Use a microscope to look at some salt and talk about whether every grain of salt will have exactly the same chemicals in it, and whether larger salt crystals will be the same chemically as smaller salt crystals. Use a microscope to look at some sand. How does this compare with salt?

The word pure is used differently in everyday speech from the way scientists use it. All elements are single pure substances containing only one type of atom. There are 94 naturally occurring elements. They are the simplest substances from which everything else is made. Salt is not an element. A compound is two or more elements chemically joined together. Pure sodium chloride (salt) is a compound because it is a molecule made of one atom of sodium (Na) chemically joined to one atom of chlorine (Cl). A mixture is made of two or more substances mixed together. These substances can be either elements or compounds. Mixtures don't always have the same amounts of each substance in them, so they can't be described as pure. Some pure substances are poisonous. Salt can be poisonous if taken in large quantities. Do you think salt is always pure? Is sea water pure? Is table salt pure? Is tap water pure? Is mineral water pure? Create a table to show the composition of different types of salt and water.

Properties of materials

4.8 Where do metals come from?

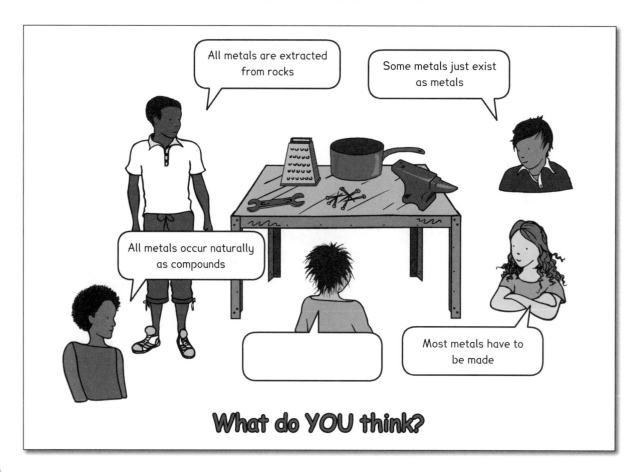

Make a list of common metals in your home. Use a textbook or the internet to find out where these metals come from. How many metals can you name? Most people can name around 10, but there are lots more! Use a periodic table to identify metals that you do not already know. Find out what arrangements your town has for recycling metals. Why do you think recycling of metals is important?

The word metal comes from the Greek word 'métallon', which means mine, quarry and metal. This suggests where most metals come from. Most metals are found in the Earth's crust. Some metals are very unreactive and can be found as pure metals. Gold is one example. People discovered and used gold more than 7 000 years ago. Most metals are more reactive than gold, and these are found in the Earth's crust as compounds called ores. The metal ores have to be mined and processed to extract the metal. If the metal is very reactive, it requires a lot of energy to extract it from its ore. Metals can also be recycled from objects made of, or containing, metals. Usually this requires less energy than extracting metals from their ores. Metals are not made. They are already present on Earth, even if extracting them from their ores can be difficult. Metals have been very important in human history. Create a table to show how different metals and their properties have influenced human civilisation over the past 5 000 years.

4.9 How is the periodic table arranged?

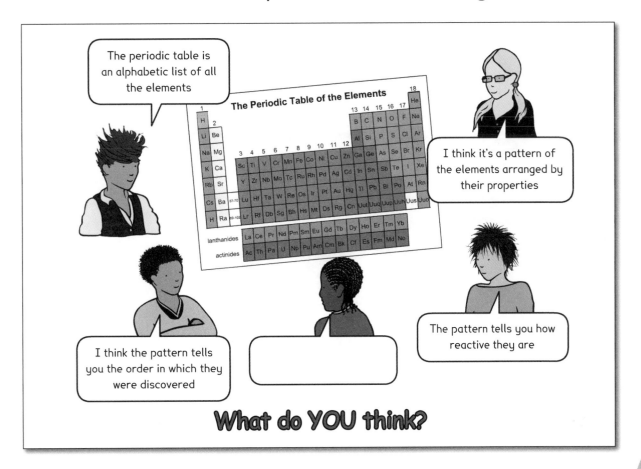

Look closely at a periodic table. Find the numbers in the corner of the element boxes. Look for any patterns in the numbering, and talk about any patterns you can spot. Find out about the history of the periodic table. Who was the first to produce one, and who created the one that we use today?

In 1869 a Russian chemist called Dmitri Mendeleev was the first scientist to create a periodic table like the one we use today. He tried to organise the elements that had already been discovered in order of the mass of each atom (the atomic mass). He realised that some elements shared similar properties, and he arranged the elements with similar properties in columns. He also predicted that not all the elements had been found, so he left gaps and predicted what properties the 'new' elements would have. As more elements were discovered his predictions were proved correct. Other scientists have used the periodic table to develop models to explain the structure of each element. They have identified the arrangement of neutrons, protons and electrons in each element to explain how they behave. Today the elements are arranged in the sequence of their atomic numbers, not their atomic mass. What is the difference between atomic number and atomic mass? Choose five elements from different parts of the periodic table, and try to explain how their atomic number and atomic mass affect the behaviour of each element.

Properties of materials

4.10 What are smart materials?

Discuss what you know about smart materials. Use the internet or reference books to look up what they are and the kind of things they can do. Find out what uses they have and how they are different from ordinary materials. If you could invent a smart material to do anything you wanted, what would it do?

Smart materials are a group of materials with special properties. Some of their properties change when an aspect of the external environment changes. For example, thermochromic materials change colour if the temperature changes (e.g. when you pour hot tea into a mug). Photochromic materials change colour if the light levels change (e.g. spectacles that go darker in sunlight). Smart materials might respond to being squashed or stretched, or to moisture, pH, electric fields, magnetic fields and so on. They might change their volume, shape, viscosity, conductivity, or other properties. Many modern devices use smart materials. Nanoparticles are different from smart materials. Nanoparticles are very tiny clusters of atoms or molecules that also have unusual properties. These properties are caused by their small size, because they have a huge surface area compared to their volume. This allows some of the properties of the individual atoms to become important, and can affect things like electrical conductivity, absorption of sunlight and melting point. They are often used to strengthen other materials or in coatings for objects to give them very hard finishes. Create a table of smart materials, what they respond to and how they respond.

Properties of materials

4.11 How reactive is gold?

Create a list of the things that are made from gold. Find out about the oldest gold objects that people have made. How old are they? Talk about what types of objects people made from gold thousands of years ago, and compare these with objects that people made from iron and bronze. Talk about the differences. Why do you think that gold has been used for hundreds of years to make crowns and artificial teeth?

Gold is one of the few metals that is found naturally on Earth. Most metals are found as compounds called ores, such as iron oxide or lead sulfide. These ores need to be processed to obtain the pure metal. The reactivity series puts metals into an order based on how reactive they are, with the most reactive at the top. The most reactive metals react rapidly and sometimes violently with water, or oxidise quickly in the air. Next there are metals that don't react with water but do react with acids. Below that are metals that only react with very strong acids. Gold is very unreactive and is at the bottom of the reactivity series, along with platinum. It reacts with a mixture of concentrated hydrochloric and nitric acids, and with elements from the halogen group, but not much else. Write a short script for a jeweller explaining to a customer why gold is a good choice for a wedding ring.

4.12 What holds atoms together?

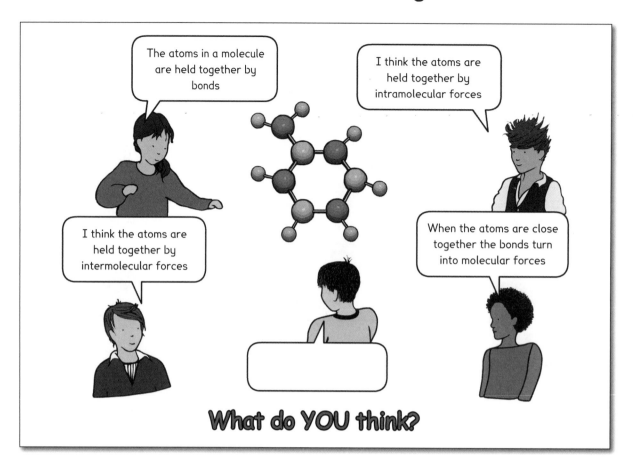

Make some models of different chemical molecules. Use a chemical model kit or modelling clay and matchsticks. Talk about what holds atoms together in your model, and how you think this compares with what holds atoms together in real molecules. Find out what the prefixes intra- and inter- mean, and discuss what this has to do with models of molecules.

When molecules are formed in reactions, some or all of the bonds between the atoms in the reactants are broken, and new bonds are formed between atoms as the products are made. Bonds are made when electrons are exchanged or shared by atoms. This changes the forces that are acting, and creates new bonds that hold the atoms together in the newly-formed molecules. The bonds between atoms in a single molecule are called intramolecular forces, and they can be very strong forces. The prefix intra- means within, so intramolecular forces are forces within the molecule. There are also forces between molecules. The prefix inter- means between, so these are called intermolecular forces. They are weaker than intramolecular forces. They hold molecules close to other molecules, as we see when molecules are arranged in a regular pattern to form crystals like sodium chloride. Use the internet to make a table of the different types of bonds that can form between atoms and molecules.

Properties of materials

4.13 How does a cold spoon get hot?

Find out what kind of kitchen utensils are used for stirring food in a pan and what they are made from. Collect several kitchen spoons made from different materials (e.g. wood, metal, plastic, silicon), put them in hot water and see what happens. Talk about where is the hottest part of the spoon and where is the coldest. What kinds of material would be good for making barbeque tongs, and why?

Safety note: the spoons may get very hot.

A metal spoon is a solid, made of particles that are packed closely together. They cannot change places or move from one end to the other. When a solid is heated the particles in it vibrate more. The higher the temperature, the more they vibrate. The particles in the spoon that are being heated vibrate more, collide with the particles next to them and make these vibrate more, and these collide with the particles next to them. The energy is transferred through the spoon by particles colliding and passing on energy to the next group of particles. This process is called conduction. The energy is in the movement of the particles, and this is not affected by gravity or the angle of the spoon. Hot gases and liquids rise in a process called convection, but this only happens in liquids and gases where the particles can move around freely. Create an annotated diagram to show how energy is transferred when sausages are being cooked in a pan.

Properties of materials

4.14 Is carbon a conductor?

Set up an investigation to find out which materials conduct electricity. Make sure you try metals, carbon, water and air. Check your results on the internet for whether each of these conducts electricity. In what way is it useful to us to know which materials conduct or don't conduct electricity?

Electricity is the flow of tiny particles called electrons that are part of all atoms. In some materials electrons can move easily, but in others they can't. The outer electrons in metal atoms are held loosely and can move in the spaces between the atoms. This means that the material can conduct electricity. These electrons are called free electrons. Carbon is not a metal, but most forms of carbon do have free electrons. Carbon conducts electricity, but not as well as a metal. Pure water doesn't have free electrons and does not conduct electricity. Most water is not pure. If it has impurities such as metal salts dissolved in it, then it conducts electricity. Electricity can travel through the air as a spark or as lightning. If you are close to high voltage cables, carrying a metal-tipped umbrella or a carbon fishing rod, a spark could jump from the cable and you could be electrocuted. Create a safety leaflet to help people understand when electrical conductors can be dangerous and why (for example, playing near railways, or getting toast out of toasters).

Properties of materials

Physical and chemical changes

5

5

Physical and chemical changes

5.1 When does water evaporate?

Pour some water into a saucer. Observe what happens if you leave it for two or three days. Does the water level change? If so, why? Compare what happens if you leave the saucer in a cool area and if you leave it in a warm area. Measure the rate of evaporation in both areas. How do hand driers work if the temperature is less than 100°C?

When a liquid gets warmer the particles in it have more energy and move faster. When particles in a liquid collide they can transfer energy from one to another. Sometimes, if the particles are close to the surface of the liquid, they have enough energy to escape from the liquid and behave as a gas. The water turns into vapour, so we say the liquid is evaporating (turning from a liquid state to gas). This can happen at any temperature, not only at 100°C, but it happens more when the liquid is warmer because the particles have more energy. Air blowing across the liquid can speed up the process by removing the water vapour and replacing it with drier air. When water boils, the water evaporates throughout the liquid and forms bubbles of water vapour that we call steam. This only happens at a specific temperature that we call the boiling point. Create an annotated drawing to show how water evaporates.

Physical and chemical changes

5.2 When does water vapour condense?

Talk about where and when you see condensation. What have you noticed about the temperature or anything else that might help to explain where the condensation comes from? Talk about when and why condensation happens in a bathroom. Talk about how you can make condensation happen. Take a can or bottle out of a fridge and see what you notice. What is the connection between condensation and rain or snow?

Condensing is when a gas turns into a liquid. Gases change state as they cool, so when water vapour (water in the form of a gas) hits a cold surface it changes into liquid water and makes tiny droplets on the cold surface. This covering of water droplets is called condensation. It happens on windows and car windscreens in winter because the glass is cold. It can also happen at a higher temperature when the air has a large amount of water vapour in it, such as in a bathroom, at a swimming pool or in a rain forest. If the surface is below 0°C, the water vapour can change directly into ice without changing into liquid water first. This is a special form of condensing called deposition. Create a poster to explain how it is possible to get condensation on the windows of an air-conditioned car on a hot day.

5.3 What happens when water freezes?

Talk together about freezing and melting and how you can test your ideas. You could weigh some ice cubes in a beaker using an accurate balance, let the ice cubes melt in a cool place, then weigh the water in the beaker. Has the mass changed? How can you check if the volume changes? Observe how ice cubes behave when you put them in water. Do they float or sink? What does that tell you about the density of ice compared to water? Observe how ice melting compares with other things that melt easily (e.g. margarine). Why is it important for plumbers to know what happens to water as it freezes?

Water is an unusual substance. Normally when a liquid solidifies, the particles get a little bit closer together and the volume gets less. The same mass is spread over a slightly smaller volume, so it is more dense and sinks if you put it in a liquid made of the same substance. Most substances do this but water doesn't. When water freezes to make ice, the volume **increases**. This means that the same mass is spread over a slightly bigger volume, so the density **decreases**. This is why ice floats on water. When ice melts its volume **decreases** but the mass doesn't change. When something melts it does not gain or lose particles so it has to be the same mass. Try to sketch an approximate graph of the volume of 100 g water from -5 to 95°C. Do some research to check your answer and find out what is special about 4°C.

5.4 What happens when things dissolve?

Try dissolving some sugar in a small amount of warm water. Observe whether the level of the water changes as you add the sugar. Check whether the mass changes. Observe whether anything else changes as the sugar dissolves. Add more sugar to the water and see what happens. Can you add as much as you want and still get it to dissolve? Does the same thing happen when you add salt to water? Can you work out whether the density of the water is changing?

When we dissolve a colourless solid in water it looks as if the solid disappears, but it is still there. We dissolve sugar in hot tea to make the tea taste sweet, so it must still be there. We cannot make or destroy the particles the sugar is made from. When we put sugar in water the volume of water initially increases. As the sugar dissolves, the crystals it is made from break down into individual particles and mix with the water, spreading in between the water particles. As the sugar particles and the water particles pack more closely together, this reduces the total volume. Also the solid sugar has air between the crystals, and this air is lost as sugar is added to the water. Therefore the total volume of the mixture is less than the volume of the sugar and the water added together. Use what you have learnt to predict what you think will happen to the volume if you mix two different liquids (e.g. water and ethanol) together and why.

Physical and chemical changes

5.5 What happens during neutralisation?

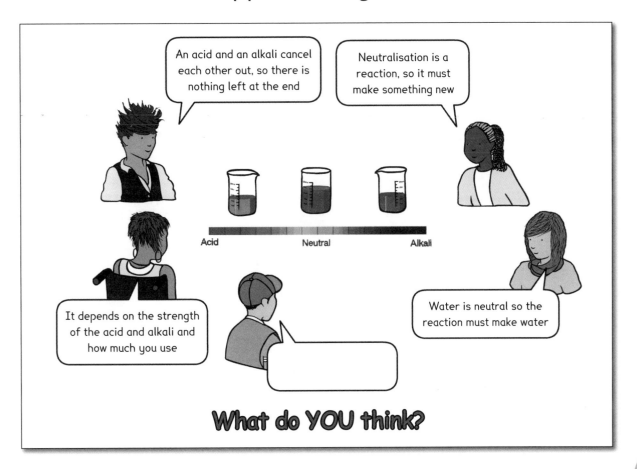

Use textbooks or the internet to find out about the pH scale. Put a small amount of a fizzy drink or apple juice in a paper cup. Use universal indicator paper to test the pH. Add a tiny amount of an antacid tablet and check the pH again. Keep adding tiny amounts of an antacid tablet and checking the pH until you reach a value of pH 7. Talk about whether what you have in the paper cup is pure water. What do you think an antacid is, and what will it do?

Safety note: Do not drink the liquid after you have tested the pH with universal indicator. It could harm you.

We sometimes think of acids and alkalis as opposites. Acids form hydrogen ions in solution and have a low pH, less than 7. Alkalis form hydroxide ions in solution and have a high pH, more than 7. If we mix the right amount of acid and alkali together they react and neutralise each other. They form a solution that is neutral with pH 7. Pure water has a pH of 7 and is not acid or alkali. However it doesn't mean there is nothing but pure water present. Neutralisation is a reaction between an acid and an alkali and the elements that made up the acid and the alkali are still there, but recombined in a different way. Equations for neutralisation look like this:

Acid + Alkali → Salt + Water

A salt is any compound that has a metal and non-metal part. The type of salt depends on which acid and which alkali were used. What advice would you give to a gardener who has soil that is too acidic to grow plants well?

5.6 What causes rusting?

Talk about the difference between elements, compounds and mixtures. Use books or the internet to check your ideas. See if you can find out what symbol is used for iron. Have a look at some rusty iron. Talk about what differences you can see between the rust and pure iron. What simple tests can you do to find out whether its properties are different? Why is it important for engineers to be able to prevent rusting?

Rusting is a chemical reaction between iron and oxygen from the air that changes the iron into iron oxide. It happens most when water is present. It is quite a slow chemical reaction so it is hard to see it happening. You need to watch a piece of damp iron for several hours to see any difference at all. When iron rusts the particles in the iron are chemically bonded to oxygen particles from the air. The iron oxide that is formed is a compound. Iron and oxygen are both elements so iron oxide cannot be an element in the periodic table. Ru in the periodic table is ruthenium, not rust. Iron oxide has different properties from pure iron, so if an iron bridge rusts it will be much weaker. Create a table to explain how the different ways of preventing rusting work.

5.7 How do elements get their symbols?

Find a copy of the periodic table and look for different types of information about it. There are some very good interactive ones on the internet. Look for numbers, letters, colours and names, and talk about any patterns that you can see. Look up sodium in a dictionary and find out why it has the symbol Na. What are the origins of some of the other symbols in the periodic table?

The periodic table is one of the most important tools chemists use to understand chemicals and chemical reactions. It has an enormous amount of information in it. The periodic table shows all the known elements, the different atoms that combine to make all the chemical compounds. There are nearly 120 known chemical elements and around 100 of these occur naturally on Earth. The symbols in the table represent the different elements and each symbol is either a capital letter on its own or a capital letter followed by a lower case letter. Na is the symbol for sodium, which is the 11th element in the table. The same symbol is used by everyone all over the world, so scientists from different countries always know what they mean even if they don't speak the same language. The symbol Na comes from the word Natrium, which is the old Latin name for sodium or sodium compounds. Create your own simplified, colour-coded version of the periodic table with a brief explanation of how it is organised.

5.8 Electrons and chemical reactions

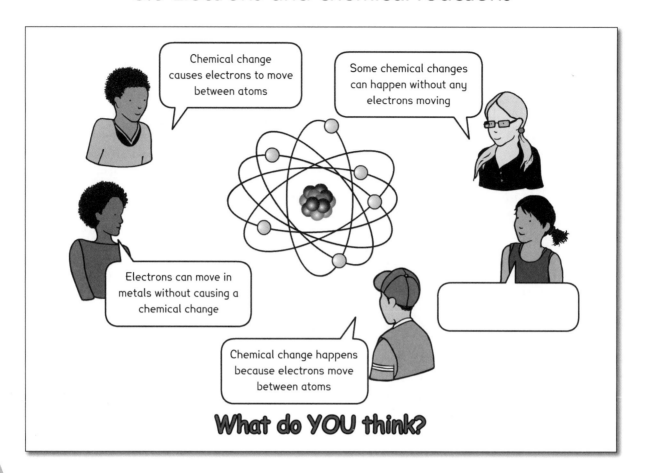

Observe some chemical reactions, such as electrolysis of water or a candle burning. What are the chemical changes, and how do you know that a chemical change is happening? Talk about what makes chemical changes different from physical changes. Do some research to find out more about electrons and chemical change. The expression valence electrons may help you. Discuss why you think groups of elements in the periodic table have similar properties and react in similar ways. What do you think would happen in an electrical circuit if the movement of electrons causes a chemical change in the metal?

Atoms are joined together by chemical bonds to form molecules. A chemical bond is formed when electrons are shared between atoms (covalent bonding) or when an electron moves from one atom to another (ionic bonding). A chemical reaction happens when new bonds, and therefore new substances, are formed. The chemical change doesn't cause the electrons to move between atoms; it happens because electrons have moved, or been shared differently, between atoms. Without this, chemical change would not happen. Metals conduct electricity because their electrons are free to move about amongst the atoms, and an electric current is the movement of these electrons. No chemical reaction takes place when the electrons flow through a metal, so metals are ideal to use in electrical circuits. Create a diagram to show what might happen to atoms and electrons when magnesium burns in air.

Physical and chemical changes

5.9 Magnesium burning

You can't easily burn your own pieces of magnesium to test this, unless you are in a laboratory. Iron wool is easier and safer to burn. Try burning a small piece of iron wool, making sure you do this safely. Talk about what you see happening and whether you think the iron wool gets heavier or lighter. Weigh it and check what has happened. Talk about whether any gases or smoke might be lost in burning and whether you can collect and weigh these. Would it be possible for something to completely disappear when it burns?

Safety note: Burning iron wool can get very hot and you might burn yourself or possibly scorch or set fire to something. Make sure you are supervised by an adult and put the iron wool on a flame-proof surface and take care with the lighter or matches you use to set it alight.

When magnesium burns it combines with oxygen from the air and makes a new substance called magnesium oxide. All the magnesium particles are still there, but each has been joined to an oxygen particle, so together they weigh more than the magnesium on its own. A chemical reaction takes place in which one set of substances, called the reactants, changes into new substances called the products. It is possible to do this in a laboratory, making sure that none of the magnesium oxide is lost, and show that it gets heavier. Some very reactive metals form oxides without having to be burnt. They just react with oxygen from the air. What advice would you give to a jewellery designer about which are the best metals to use, which metals would not be suitable, and why?

Physical and chemical changes

5.10 Numbers in equations

Look up some equations in chemistry textbooks or on the internet. Talk about what the numbers in the equations might mean. Use the periodic table to help you. Use a book or the internet to check what the symbols and numbers represent. How do you think scientists know how many atoms there are in a reaction when atoms are much too small to be seen?

Elements are the atoms that join together to make more complicated molecules. They are listed in the periodic table. Because of the way the electrons in each atom are arranged, atoms only combine in certain ways. For example, every water molecule is a combination of two hydrogen atoms and one oxygen atom, giving it a formula H_2O. When magnesium burns it makes magnesium oxide. Each atom of magnesium combines with one atom of oxygen to make magnesium oxide, MgO. Correctly written chemical equations must balance, with the same numbers of each atom on each side. Oxygen in the air is a molecule made from two oxygen atoms joined together, with a formula O_2. Because oxygen is always found as O_2 we have to show that one molecule (two atoms) of oxygen reacts with two atoms of magnesium to make two molecules of magnesium oxide. The small numbers show the number of atoms in each molecule, and the large numbers show how many molecules there are. Make some models or pictures of the atoms to explain the equation to someone else.

98

5.11 Temperature change in reactions

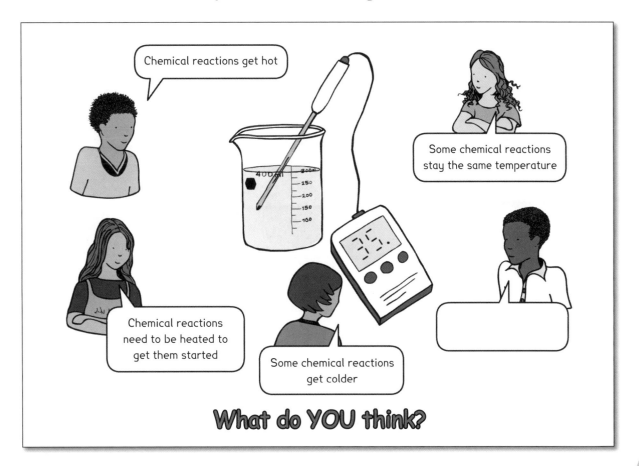

Talk about some chemical reactions that you have seen. Do any of them get hot or cold? Mix some baking soda with vinegar and record the temperature. Find out whether the temperature changes as they react. Can you explain what is happening? What do you think exothermic and endothermic mean?

Chemical reactions involve a change in energy. Some chemical reactions get hot. For example, when something burns, a chemical reaction takes place where oxygen reacts with the fuel and releases energy as the chemicals combine. Putting some metals in acid causes a reaction that gets hot. Some reactions absorb energy. For example, if you react ethanoic acid (vinegar) with sodium hydrogen carbonate (baking soda), the temperature goes down. Energy is removed from the surroundings to make the reaction happen. Some reactions need to be at a high temperature to get started, but then they release energy and keep going by themselves, like burning magnesium. Some reactions don't involve any noticeable change in temperature. What kinds of energy changes take place in preparing and cooking food? Create a list of examples.

5.12 Exothermic/endothermic reactions

Light a small candle and watch it burn. Concentrate on the flame. Talk about what is happening in terms of energy transfer – what changes are taking place, how does the flame carry on burning, where does the energy come from and where does it end up? How can you tell if a chemical reaction is happening? Look this up in a book or on the internet if you are not sure.

Safety note: A candle flame is very hot and you could burn yourself or possibly scorch or set fire to something. Make sure you are supervised by an adult, that the candle is securely on a flame-proof surface and cannot fall over. Take care with the lighter or matches you use to light it.

In a chemical reaction, some bonds between atoms and molecules are broken and new bonds are formed. Energy is needed to break the bonds and start the chemical reaction. This is called the activation energy. Sometimes the activation energy is so low that the reaction starts spontaneously. This is because the energy of the particles colliding is enough to start the reaction. Once it starts, burning is an exothermic reaction. This means that energy is transferred to the surroundings. The flame burns at a fairly constant temperature and transfers energy to the surroundings. Some reactions are endothermic, which means they need to absorb energy to happen. These reactions often need to be heated to work, and they make the surroundings colder. Making an omelette from raw eggs is an endothermic reaction. You have to put in energy to make this reaction happen. Can you make a list of what you think are the five most important exothermic and endothermic reactions that affect your everyday life? Does everyone agree?

100

Electricity and magnetism

6

Electricity and magnetism

6.1 Power or energy — which?

Is power a noun, a verb or an adjective? Use an ordinary dictionary to look it up. Now check the definition in a science dictionary or textbook and see whether you get the same definition. Can you think of any words that have one definition in everyday speech and a more specific definition in science?

Power is a word that is commonly used in everyday speech but has a very specific meaning in science. Scientists use the word power to mean the amount of energy transferred per unit of time. Energy is the measure of how much work has been done, but it doesn't tell you anything about how quickly. Energy is measured in joules (J), where one joule is the work done in applying a force of one newton through one metre. Power is measured in watts (W), where one watt is the same as one joule per second (J/s). Joules and watts can also be used to describe electrical power and energy. The company National Power is using one of the everyday uses of the word power to describe how energy is provided by electricity, such as 'My computer is powered by electricity'. Write a short paragraph about a weightlifter (or some other athlete) to illustrate the difference between power and energy.

6.2 How can birds sit on power lines?

Look at some photographs of birds' feet. Talk about whether they might be made from rubber and how rubber feet might be useful to a bird. Discuss how you can get an electric shock, and what might be different for the bird on the wire. Sometimes electricity companies put marker buoys on power lines to make them more visible where there are lots of large birds in the area. If birds can sit on power lines, why do you think the marker buoys are useful?

An electric current flowing through your body will give you an electric shock. For a current to flow, there needs to be a difference in voltage to push the current and a complete circuit for it to flow round. Birds can perch on an electrical wire because both their feet are at the same voltage, and the electricity cannot flow to earth because there is no complete circuit for it to flow through. This means that the electricity cannot flow. If a bird has one leg on the ground and the other on a wire, the circuit will be completed because the electricity can flow through them to earth, so it will be electrocuted. If it has a leg on one wire and a part of its body touches a second wire at a different voltage, the same thing will happen. Make a list of the dangers engineers who inspect live 400kV overhead cables might experience and how you think they overcome these dangers.

Electricity and magnetism

6.3 Is current used up in a circuit?

Try wiring a circuit with two lamps in series. Predict what will happen if you add a third lamp to the circuit. Try it. Use an ammeter to measure the current at different points in the circuit. If you can't make a real circuit, there are electrical circuit simulations on the internet. Christmas tree lights used to be wired in series. Why do you think manufacturers stopped wiring them like this?

For a lamp to light it must be a part of a complete circuit. This allows electrons to flow around the circuit, transferring energy from the power source to the lamp. Each component in a circuit resists the flow of electricity, and this resistance determines how much current flows at any voltage. The current flows in one direction. Scientists used to think that positive charges flow from the positive end of the battery towards the negative. Now they think that negative charges (electrons) flow from the negative end towards the positive. When the components are wired in series the electrons can follow only one path, flowing through each of the lamps. Each lamp has the same amount of current flowing though it, so they have the same amount of energy transferred to them and are equally bright. If one lamp breaks, no more electrons can flow and none of the lamps will light. Make a comparison table to show the advantages and disadvantages of using series or parallel circuits in the home.

Electricity and magnetism

6.4 Different models of electricity

Draw a picture of a simple electric circuit. Add notes to your picture to explain how you think it works. Now try to make connections between your picture of a circuit and a helter skelter, a hosepipe, a bicycle chain and someone delivering letters. You can find ideas to help you on the internet. Which model is easiest to connect with your picture? How could a central heating system be used as a model of an electric circuit?

We use models in science to help us to understand ideas. Electricity can be difficult to understand because we cannot see how it works. There are lots of models to help us to think about electricity. Each model is good at explaining some observations, but not so good at explaining others. The hosepipe model helps to explain the flow of electrons in a current in the wire. The helter skelter model helps to explain the idea of voltage and energy transfer as the person slides from the top to the bottom. Someone delivering letters helps to explain the idea that the current carries energy and transfers some energy to each place it visits. The bicycle chain explains that the current is not used up and energy is transferred from the battery to the components. Make a comparison table for someone who has never heard of these models to show what they explain well and what they don't explain.

Electricity and magnetism

6.5 When a generator speeds up ...

Set up a circuit with a lamp, using either a hand-held generator or a static cycle with a dynamo as a power source. Use your model circuit to explore what happens to the lamp when you pedal faster. Use a voltmeter to measure the voltage as you pedal. Discuss what this tells you about what is happening to the current and voltage as you pedal faster. How does Michael Faraday's work link with generators and help you to understand how they work?

A bicycle can generate electricity if it is used to turn a generator. If the cyclist pedals faster, the generator will turn faster and more voltage will be produced. The voltage makes electrons move, so the increased voltage makes more electrons move and therefore there is more current. The person cycling doesn't make extra electrons or increase the charge on the electrons; the electrons are charged particles that are in the copper wires already. The electrons don't move faster or slower, but more of them move. As the voltage pushes the current through a component like a lamp it has to do work, and some energy is transferred from the electrons to the lamp. When the current is bigger there are more electrons to transfer energy, so a high current will make a lamp shine brighter than a low current. Create an illustration using a simple model of electricity (see Concept Cartoon 6.4) to explain the difference that pedalling faster makes.

Electricity and magnetism

6.6 What is voltage?

Look at some different batteries and find out what voltage they supply. Find out the voltage for the electricity supply to your home. Look up voltage in a science dictionary or on the internet to see how it is described and what its effects are. How do the chemicals inside a battery affect the voltage?

Voltage is defined as the amount of energy needed to move one unit of charge between two points in a circuit. The voltage of a battery (or cell) tells us how much electromotive force is available to push the electrons, causing them to flow in a current round the circuit. It is caused by a difference in potential between two parts of a circuit and is sometimes called potential difference. The more voltage there is, the more electrons flow round the circuit and the bigger the current is. If we think of electric current as being like water flowing in a pipe, voltage is the pump that provides the pressure to push the water along. Chemical reactions in a battery provide the energy to produce the voltage that moves electrons round the circuit. Eventually the chemical reactions can't occur because the reactants have been used up, so the voltage drops to zero and no more current flows. High-voltage batteries tend to be bigger than lower-voltage ones, but you can't tell the voltage just by looking at the size of the battery. The chemicals inside the battery make a difference. Create a Wikipedia-style explanation of voltage to help other people understand what it is.

108

6.7 Does the size of a battery matter?

Use a computer program to set up a model circuit. Use this to find out what happens when you increase the voltage. Check this with a real circuit if you can. Measuring the current with an ammeter when you change the voltage will help you to understand what is happening. Look at some advertisements for 6v batteries. What is different about the different types that are available?

In this example the lamp produces the right amount of light with a 3v battery. A 6v battery produces twice as much current in this circuit as a 3v battery, so the lamp will be brighter and the filament in the lamp may melt. Using the wrong voltage may cause damage to electrical equipment because it produces a bigger current. The physical size of the battery doesn't tell you how much voltage it produces, so a 6v battery won't necessarily be twice the size of a 3v one and it may not last twice as long. If you set up a circuit with a 6v battery it will light twice as many lamps to their usual brightness as a 3v battery. Two lamps in series need twice the voltage of one lamp on its own to get the same current flowing through them. Why do you think there are so many different types of batteries? Make a list of what manufacturers need to consider when they choose a battery for a device.

6.8 Why do wires get hot?

Make some toast in a toaster. You should see the element glowing red hot. Make a list of other electrical devices that get hot to cook food or heat things. Make another list of electrical devices that are not designed to cook food or heat things, even if they get warm when they are switched on. Find out about a device containing a wire that is designed to melt when a big current goes through it. How does it work? Do some research to find out why wires can get hot when an electric current passes through them.

Safety note: The element in a toaster can get very hot and you might burn yourself. Make sure you are supervised by an adult when you try this out. NEVER push or poke anything into the heating element of the toaster. The bare wires are live and you could get a very bad electric shock.

Current is a flow of electrons. The current flows because a voltage pushes the electrons through the wire. The wire resists the flow of the electrons as they collide with metal atoms in the wire. A thinner and longer wire has more resistance. The current flowing through a wire makes it get warmer because of the wire's resistance. The bigger the current is, the hotter the wire gets. The wire in the toaster is the right length and thickness to have enough resistance to get red hot when the current flows. The wire leading to the toaster is much thicker, and is made to have very little resistance, so it doesn't get hot. The insulation on the wire is there to prevent anybody getting a shock, not because it gets hot. The voltage, current and resistance are all related by Ohms law. How can a fuse wire (or circuit breaker) help to make sure that a toaster is safe to use? Create a report to share your ideas.

Electricity and magnetism

6.9 Electricity and magnetism

Use a textbook or the internet to find out about the discoveries of Hans Christian Oersted, William Sturgeon, Andre-Marie Ampere and Michael Faraday. Discuss how their discoveries help you to understand how electricity and magnetism might be connected. Which electrical devices do you have in your home that use magnets? How do electricity and magnetism work together in these devices?

Electricity and magnetism are closely connected. Motors, dynamos, generators and electromagnets all work because of this connection. Electricity can create a magnetic field, and magnetism can create an electric current. A wire with an electric current flowing through it has a magnetic field around it. If the wire is coiled up the fields add together and become stronger. If a soft iron core is put in the middle the magnetism is concentrated and becomes even stronger than before. When the electricity stops flowing, the soft iron stops being a magnet. Electric motors use coils of wire and magnets to make them move when a current passes through them. Generators work the other way, and use coils of wire and magnets to make electric currents when they are moved. Some devices like solar cells can make electricity without using a magnet, but most of our electricity comes from generators that use magnets or electromagnets. Draw a diagram to show what you think the electric circuit in an electric bell or a magnetic door lock is like. Share it with others. Do they agree?

6.10 Is magnetism used up?

Magnetise an iron nail by stroking it in one direction with one end of a strong magnet. Find a way to measure how strong your new magnet is. Does the magnet that you started with get weaker when you make a new magnet? Does the number of times you stroke it affect the strength of the new magnet?

Magnets are made by placing a magnetic material near a very strong electromagnet. Some materials, such as iron, steel, cobalt and nickel, become magnetic more easily than others. The groups of atoms inside them are like tiny magnets. They line up with the magnetic field of the electromagnet. The magnetism from each group of atoms adds together to make up the magnetism of the whole magnet. A magnet can lose some of its magnetism if the groups of atoms get out of line. This can happen if it is kept near other magnets, gets too hot or is hit or vibrated a lot. You can make a magnet by stroking a piece of steel in the same direction with one end of a permanent magnet. This lines up the groups of atoms in the steel and makes it a weak magnet. The magnetism hasn't been passed on to the steel and it doesn't get used up. If modern magnets are kept carefully they will stay magnetic forever. When you buy magnets they often come with 'keepers'. Find out what these are and draw how you think they might work.

Electricity and magnetism

6.11 If you break a magnet ...

Get an iron nail and use a saw to cut partway through it. Make it into a magnet by stroking it in one direction with a permanent magnet. See how many paper clips it picks up. Now break it in half and investigate the two separate pieces. What do you find? Put two bar magnets together so that the ends attract each other. What are the properties of this double-size magnet?

Magnetic materials, like iron, have groups of atoms in them that have magnetic properties. These regions are called domains. The motion of the electrons in these domains creates a magnetic field and the domains are like little magnets. If all the domains line up in the same direction the whole material becomes a magnet. Magnets can be made by stroking a piece of iron with a strong magnet, so all the domains in the iron line up in the same direction. If the domains are not lined up the magnetism is weak or non-existent. The magnetism only changes if the atoms in the domains are rearranged. Cutting a magnet in half does not change the way the domains are lined up, so each half acts like a magnet. However there are fewer domains in each half, so each half is weaker than the whole magnet. The magnetic domains each have a north and south pole so it isn't possible to get one pole on its own. Scientists are investigating making tiny magnets out of single atoms. What can you find out about this? Share your ideas for creative uses for nanomagnets.

113

6.12 What are magnetic field lines?

Get some iron filings in a clear plastic envelope and shake them around a magnet. Discuss what patterns you can see. Check what you see on the internet or in a textbook. Put two magnets close together and shake iron filings around them. What happens when the magnetism from the two magnets meet? How is magnetism different from a force like friction? What other field forces can you find out about?

Safety note: Don't use loose iron filings - they can cause serious damage if they get into your eyes. Only use them when they are sealed in a container or packet.

There is an invisible magnetic field around any magnet. The strength of the field depends on the distance from the magnet. Scientists use magnetic field lines to show how strong the field is, but they don't really exist. The field lines are drawn close together to show where the field is strong, and far apart where the field is weak. They are like contour lines on a map, that show how high something is but don't exist in real life. The magnetic force is everywhere around the magnet, not just where the lines are drawn. Iron filings in the magnetic field act like little magnets. When they can move a bit they are attracted to the other filings and line up like a string of tiny magnets, but they are not following any real lines. Sometimes the Earth is said to be like a giant magnet. Draw a picture to show what the Earth's magnetic field is like, and create a list of reasons why this is important to us. Write a newspaper report about what might happen if this magnetic field disappears.

Electricity and magnetism

6.13 Fuses and earth wires

With the help of an adult, find an old electric plug and look at the wiring inside it. Check what colour the wires are. Find out what each of the different wires is called and what it does. Look up a diagram of a plug in a textbook or on the internet. Check what the other parts of the plug are. Identify where the fuse is and what it looks like. Find out where the electrical trip switches or fuse box are in your house and get someone to show them to you.

Earth wires, fuses and trip switches are designed to keep you safe from an electric shock. The earth wire is connected to the case of the appliance and, through the plug and wiring in the house, directly to the ground. If a fault develops and the case becomes live, the electricity has an easy path to follow, through the earth wire, to the ground. This causes a very large current to flow. If this happens the fuse very quickly heats up and melts, cutting the electricity off and making it safe. Trip switches work in a different way. They measure the current flowing into a circuit and the current flowing back out. These should always be equal because current isn't used up in a circuit. If there is a difference some current has been able to leave the circuit, probably because of a fault, so the trip switch automatically cuts the electrical supply off. Trip switches work faster than earth wires and fuses so they are safer. Create a safety leaflet for householders to show how earth wires, fuses and trip switches work.

6.14 Complicated house wiring

Talk about how a light switch is connected to a lamp. Talk about what kind of circuit is needed to control a lamp with two switches in different parts of a house. Try to build this circuit using wires or model it using a computer programme. In the UK a system known as a ring circuit (ring main) is used. Can you find out why it was introduced?

House wiring is complicated and should only be touched by an expert. Houses have different circuits. Some circuits control the lights, some control sockets, and some appliances like cookers have their own circuit because of the amount of current they need. We should be able to turn on each socket while other sockets stay off, and each appliance has to be independently controlled by switches without affecting the other appliances. That means each socket and appliance needs separate wiring. In a typical house there are many hundreds of wires connecting switches, lights and sockets. All the circuits are controlled by fuses or circuit breakers. The circuits we create to learn about electricity are much simpler than real house wiring. These simple circuits generally use low-voltage direct current (DC) which only flows in one direction. Houses run on higher-voltage alternating current (AC), which constantly changes direction, going first one way then the other up to 50 or 60 times a second. Sketch a simplified circuit diagram to show a householder what the electric circuits in their house will look like.

Electricity and magnetism

6.15 What is static electricity?

Rub a balloon with a cloth and see what happens if you put it next to your hair or some small pieces of tissue. Try different cloths, and see if it makes any difference. Try rubbing different plastics (e.g. a plastic ruler) to see if the same thing happens. Look up static electricity on the internet or in a book. Why do you think we don't use static electricity in circuits?

Static electricity is created when charges are transferred from one object to another. Electrons are transferred when you rub a balloon with some types of cloth. The build up of electrical charge is what we call static electricity. It creates effects like making your hair stand up or making tissue stick to a balloon. Small amounts of static charge don't do any damage to you. Lightning is an electrostatic discharge that can happen when a cloud becomes charged with static electricity. Clouds become charged when ice crystals and slushy water are blown about and collide inside the cloud. The lighter ice crystals become positively charged and collect at the top of the cloud, and heavier slushy water and hail become negatively charged and collect at the bottom. If enough charge builds up there is a discharge in the form of lightning, either inside the cloud, between clouds, or from the cloud to the ground. This can be very damaging. Static electricity can also be generated in some materials by pressure or heat. Create a storyboard sequence to show how you think the movement of negative electrons can make an object positively charged.

117

6.16 What are force fields?

Use the internet or textbooks to find out about force fields. Talk about what types of forces have fields, and how many types of force fields there are. Talk about the difference between forces that act through contact and force fields. How do you think a magnet attracts a paperclip without touching it?

There are three basic types of force fields: gravitational fields, electric fields and magnetic fields. Force fields allow forces to act at a distance without anything touching. Most people are familiar with magnetic force fields. If you try to push two north magnetic poles together you can feel the force repelling them, and it is difficult to get them to touch. Gravity is a force field that we experience all the time. It is caused by the mass of the Earth interacting with other objects, and it is strong enough to keep us on the ground and to keep the Moon in its orbit. All objects with mass create a gravitational field around them. Electric fields are created by electrical charges. When objects touch, any force between them is caused by the repulsion of the electric fields of the atoms at their surfaces. Electric fields are therefore responsible for the common contact forces (pushes and pulls) that we experience every day. Create a set of annotated drawings to show the difference between forces acting through contact and forces acting at a distance.

Electricity and magnetism

Forces, energy resources and energy transfer

7

7

Forces, energy resources & energy transfer

7.1 Does weight change in water?

Use a forcemeter to weigh a 1 kg mass in air. Now lower it into a tank of water, and weigh it again while it is partly submerged and when it is completely under the water. Feel what happens when you push a balloon under the surface of the water. Talk about what this tells you about a person's weight in air and water. How do you think the forcemeter reading would change if you lower a large block of wood into a tank of water?

Weight is the force of gravity that pulls on an object due to its mass. It is measured in Newtons, like all other forces. If you put an object in water its mass does not change. Gravity pulls on it with the same force, so its weight is the same as well, but another force becomes important. As you lower an object into water it pushes some water out of the way. The water surrounding the object pushes back. This 'pushing back' force is called buoyancy. You can feel this force as you lower yourself into water when you go swimming. The force is just big enough to keep you floating at the surface. The combination of gravity and buoyancy means that things seem to weigh less in water than in air. Objects that are more dense than water also have a buoyancy, but the buoyancy force is less than their weight, so these objects do not float. Ships are usually made of steel and steel is much denser than water. Use annotated diagrams to explain to someone how a steel boat can float.

121

7.2 Are weight and pressure the same?

Use weighing scales to find out what happens if you weigh yourself standing on one leg. Weigh a wooden or metal bar using electronic scales. Now balance the bar on two scales and take the reading on each of them. Talk about what you observe and how this helps you to understand the connection between mass, weight and pressure. What will happen to the pressure if a person wears stiletto heels?

Weight is the force of gravity that pulls on an object due to its mass. It is measured in Newtons, like all other forces. Standing on one leg or two doesn't change your weight. Weighing scales measure how much force you press down on them with, due to gravity. Even though the units on the scales refer to Kilograms, it is the force your mass pushes down with that is being measured, not your mass. If you stand on two scales, one foot on each, each scale takes about half the force and reads about half as much, but if you add them together your mass and weight have not changed. Pressure tells us how spread out a force is and is measured in N/m^2 (Newtons per square metre). If you stand on one foot, all your weight is concentrated into half the area of two feet, so the pressure will double. Draw a force diagram to show how snowshoes can stop you sinking into deep snow in the winter.

7.3 Does the strength of a bridge vary?

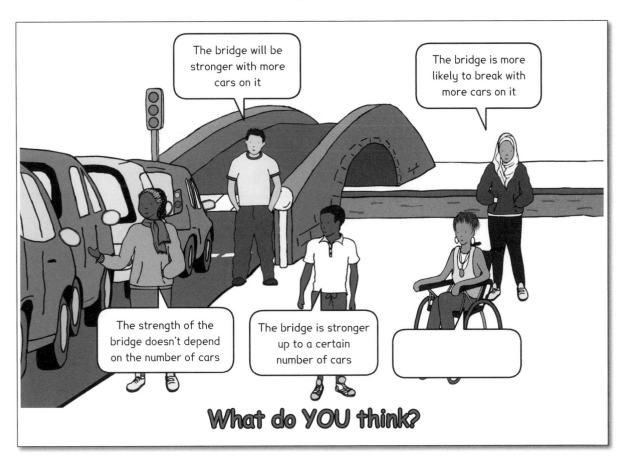

Do an internet search for images of Roman bridges that still exist today. What pattern do you notice in how they are constructed? Make some simple model bridges out of card and test them to see what load they can support. Try different shapes and find out which shapes are the strongest. If some shapes are stronger than others, why do you think that all bridges aren't the same shape?

Arched bridges have been around for thousands of years. This is because the shape is very strong. Some of the stones or bricks they are built from are wedge-shaped and laid with the thicker part towards the top. The weight of things on the bridge pushes them together, locks them in place and makes the bridge even stronger. They resist being compressed really well. The shape transfers the weight of the cars on the bridge to the ground on either side. If the bridge becomes really overloaded, the stones or bricks can start to crack and break up. If enough of them do this then the bridge can become weaker and collapse. Modern bridges are built using steel and reinforced concrete, which have different properties to stone. This allows different shapes and designs to be used. How do other types of bridges transfer forces to the ground? Draw some force diagrams to show how different-shaped bridges can support a load.

7.4 Are forces balanced?

Ride a bike on a flat surface. Check what happens to the speed when you stop pedalling. What happens when you ride it on different surfaces or with flat tyres? What happens when you stop pedalling going downhill? If you don't have access to a bike, push a small model car instead. Talk about what forces must be involved to explain your observations. How do Newton's Laws help with your explanations?

Forces can act in different directions. Their effects add together if they are in the same direction, and subtract from each other if they are in opposite directions. Equal and opposite forces can balance each other out so the object can act as if there is no force on it. A bike travelling at a constant speed has no overall force acting on it. There are lots of forces acting, but there are two main forces to consider – the force from pedalling that pushes the bike forwards, and the force of friction (from the road and the air resistance) that pushes against it. If the bike is going at a constant speed then these forces must be balanced. If they are not balanced then the bike will speed up or slow down. How would you explain to someone how the forces acting on a bike travelling at constant speed are different from the forces acting when it is speeding up or slowing down?

Forces, energy resources & energy transfer

7.5 How does sliding affect friction?

Try pushing a heavy trolley on wheels, or a heavy box on rollers. Use a forcemeter to find out how much force is needed to get it moving and to keep it moving. Which force is biggest? Talk about where you think these forces come from. Why do you think marbles or polystyrene granules make things move more easily?

Friction is a force that opposes motion. It always works in the opposite direction to the movement or attempted movement of an object. It is usually caused by roughness (sometimes at molecular level) on the surfaces of the objects. There are several types of friction but in this example there are only two types acting, static friction and kinetic friction. Static friction acts when an object is in contact with another object but they are not moving. The cat can sit on a sloping surface and not slide down if the static friction is big enough to balance the force of gravity pulling it down the slope. If the roof is slippery, or if the slope is steep, then the force from gravity may be greater than the static friction, and the cat slides. Kinetic friction happens as one object moves across the surface of another. When the cat is moving the friction is only kinetic friction. Kinetic friction is almost always smaller than static friction, so the greatest friction occurs just before the object starts to move. Create a chart to show when friction can be helpful to people and when it is unhelpful.

Forces, energy resources & energy transfer

7.6 What happens if you throw a ball?

Weigh different balls and see how far you can throw them. Talk about whether there is any relationship between the mass of the balls and how far they can be thrown. Do you use the same force each time you throw the ball? Would some sort of launcher help? What else might affect how far you can throw the ball?

When a force is used to accelerate a ball, the acceleration is directly related to its mass. If you halve the mass of the ball, the same force produces twice the acceleration. When the ball is moving air resistance becomes important. The faster the ball goes, the greater the force of friction between it and the air, and this slows the ball down. If the speed of the ball is doubled, the friction increases four times as much (that's 2 squared which = 4), not twice as much. Getting things to go really fast is difficult because of this relationship between speed and air resistance. When the ball is thrown harder it goes faster and further. The exact distance it travels depends on air resistance, the angle it is thrown at and on whether it is spinning, as this can change its path through the air. Predicting exactly what will happen is difficult. Air resistance has the same effect on a moving car as on a moving ball. Sketch a graph to show how you think fuel consumption will change as a car's speed changes. Check your answers using a reference source.

Forces, energy resources & energy transfer

7.7 Does a surface push upwards?

Sit on a hard chair and do a thought experiment. What would happen if the chair wasn't there? Can you feel the chair pushing up on you? How does the chair know how much force to push up with? What do you think is happening to the atoms in the chair? What happens if you push down with more force than the chair can support?

If we drop an object, it falls to the ground because of gravity. If we hang it on a spring it doesn't fall to the ground. Gravity pulls it towards the Earth with a force equal to its weight, but now the spring holds it up. There is a force in the spring pulling the object upwards, equal to the force pulling it down. If we put a laptop on a table it doesn't fall to the ground because an upwards force from the table holds it up. The top few layers of atoms in the table get slightly squashed by the laptop and the bonds between them get compressed. The bonds act like tiny springs, resisting the push and pushing back as they are compressed. All the bonds between the atoms pushing back create a force that balances the weight of the laptop. A heavier object on the table makes the bonds compress more and push back with more force, so the force from the table balances the weight of the object. Draw a series of diagrams to show the forces in a trampoline when a heavy object is placed on it.

127

7.8 What forces act in stretching?

Use both hands to stretch an elastic band. Feel how the elastic band pulls your hands. Observe what happens if you let one end go suddenly. Find out what happens if you try to pull one end with more force than the other. Talk about how Newton's Laws help you to understand what is happening. If action and reaction are equal and opposite, how can one side ever win in a tug of war?

Safety note: if stretching an elastic band, use a small one to avoid any risk of hurting yourself.

To make a bungee stretch, you need to have equal and opposite forces at each end. If you attach one end to a wall, when you pull the force is transferred through the bungee to the wall. The atoms in the wall get pulled a tiny bit further apart, and the bonds that hold them together get stretched and provide a force that resists the pull (a bit like a spring does). By doing this the whole wall pulls on the bungee with a force equal and opposite to the force at the end being pulled. This makes the bungee stretch. As the bungee stretches, the atoms that make it up get pulled further apart, and the bonds get stretched and provide a force that resists the pull in both directions. You and the wall pull on the bungee, and the bungee pulls back on you and the wall. Use these ideas to work out what happens when you drop a tennis ball onto the ground. Draw some diagrams to illustrate how the tennis ball responds in this situation.

Forces, energy resources & energy transfer

7.9 Is temperature the same as heat?

Use a thermometer to take the temperatures of different things around you. Hold a thermometer gently between your hands and notice what happens to the temperature. Talk about what must be happening for the temperature reading to change. Find out the difference between 0° Fahrenheit, 0° Celcius and 0° Kelvin. Is there anywhere where the temperature is absolute zero? How does blowing on your hands warm them up in the winter and cool them down in the summer?

Temperature, heat, hot and cold are words we use everyday, but we don't always use them as precisely as scientists do. Heating is a process of transferring energy from one thing to another. When you heat water in an electric kettle, energy is transferred by electricity to become energy stored in the water. The temperature of the water goes up as we heat it, and this tells us how much energy we have transferred to the water. Hot and cold are words we use to describe the difference in temperatures between different places. A fridge is cold compared to a room, and a freezer is cold compared to a fridge. We use temperature in everyday speech to tell us how hot or cold something is because we usually assume that we are comparing something to room temperature or our body temperature – e.g. a cold day, or a hot cup of tea. It is more accurate to think of temperature as a measure of the amount of energy something has. Create a Wikipedia-style entry to explain heat and temperature, including a temperature of absolute zero.

Forces, energy resources & energy transfer

7.10 Does size affect cooling?

Cook some potatoes in boiling water or an oven. Cook a small potato, a large potato and another large potato to mash after it is cooked. See how quickly each of them goes cold. Talk about how to explain your results in terms of energy transfer. Can you predict how quickly a large block of ice, an ice cube and crushed ice will melt, and why?

Safety note: Cooking potatoes needs to be supervised by an adult. Cooked potatoes will be hot. Boiling water can cause serious burns.

When an object cools, energy is transferred from its surface by conduction, convection and radiation. When the surface becomes cooler than the centre, energy flows towards the surface by conduction. This continues until the object has transferred enough energy to be at the same temperature as the surroundings. The size of the surface area influences how quickly energy is lost. A bigger surface area allows energy be transferred more easily. A round object has less surface area than a thin flat object with the same volume, so it transfers energy more slowly. It has a smaller surface to volume ratio. Small potatoes and mashed potatoes have a bigger surface to volume ratio than large potatoes, so they transfer energy more easily and their temperature falls more quickly. The same is true of animals. A mouse has a bigger surface to volume ratio than an elephant, so it transfers energy more quickly. Draw some pictures to show the problems that large and small animals have in terms of energy transfer in very cold or very hot climates.

Forces, energy resources & energy transfer

7.11 Does stirring make liquids cooler?

Try stirring tea that is at different temperatures. Use a datalogger and temperature probe to measure the temperature of the tea. Does it get hotter, colder or stay the same? Does the same thing happen with other liquids? Do some research to check your ideas and find out what might be happing to the particles in the liquid. You blow on your hands in the winter to warm them, so how can blowing on a hot drink cool it down?

Safety note: use caution with hot liquids.

The particles in a hot drink have a lot of energy and move about very quickly. As they move about they heat their surroundings and transfer some of their energy. The cooler the air around them is, the faster they transfer their energy to the air. The liquid at the surface transfers some of its energy to the air particles above the liquid, and this makes the liquid cooler and the air warmer, so the rate of energy transfer slows down. Stirring the drink moves the cooler liquid particles away from the surface, and moves warmer liquid particles to the surface. It also moves the warmer air particles away from the surface of the liquid, replacing them with cooler air. This means that the stirred liquid can transfer more of its energy to the air, so the drink cools down faster. What sort of shape might minimise energy transfer and keep a drink warmer for longer? Design a coffee cup based on your ideas.

Forces, energy resources & energy transfer

7.12 Can energy be destroyed?

Talk about why you think it is important to switch off lights when they are not in use. Find out how much energy a light bulb uses and how much it costs to run for an hour. Do some research to find out why some light bulbs are called energy saving and use much less electricity than others. What do you think people mean when they talk about energy conservation?

Energy cannot be made or destroyed; it is just transferred from one place to another. As it is transferred it can do work for us. In this case the work is the lighting we use to see with. The energy a lamp emits just before it is switched off is not destroyed. Some of it is carried away into space by light, but most is absorbed by the surroundings, causing them to get very slightly warmer. The power station transfers energy from the fossil fuel into electricity, but it doesn't create any energy. Turning lamps off saves money on your electricity bill, but there are other important reasons to save electricity. All over the world a lot of electricity is generated by burning fossil fuels in a power station, and this makes CO_2 which causes problems when it is released into the atmosphere. Reducing the electricity we use reduces the CO_2 we make. Create a poster to encourage people to conserve energy.

Forces, energy resources & energy transfer

7.13 How is energy dissipated?

Set up a circuit with a lamp and a buzzer inside a shoe box. Use a datalogger and sensors to record the light level, sound level and temperature when the light and buzzer are switched on. Talk about the data you collect. Do you think red, blue and white light will raise the temperature by the same amount? Talk about this and check your answer on the internet (look for William Herschel the astronomer).

When the disco starts, energy is transferred to the surroundings by sound and light. The light gets absorbed by the different surfaces in the room, and they get slightly warmer. The sound makes the windows, doors and walls vibrate more, and they get slightly warmer. These energy transfers cause the temperature of the room to rise by a small amount. This is difficult to measure as the temperature difference is so small. People dancing in the room use their muscles and get hotter, so a lot of energy is transferred into the room, making the temperature of the room rise noticeably. Think about how the temperature of a classroom gets higher when it is full of students, even when they are not dancing! Some of the sound can also travel through the windows, doors and walls into the environment beyond the room. Draw a picture to show what you think happens to the light and sound when a firework explodes.

7.14 Colour and energy absorption

Talk about whether dressing in black or white on a hot summer day makes a difference to how hot you feel. How does it feel when you get into a black or a white car on a hot summer day? Use temperature probes inside two shoe boxes, painted black or white, to model what happens to the temperature inside a black or white car on a hot summer day. Why do you think houses in very hot countries are usually painted white?

The colour of a solar panel makes a difference because black surfaces absorb more energy than white surfaces. The reason that a black surface appears black is because it absorbs light rather than reflecting light. As it absorbs light radiation (especially infrared radiation) its temperature increases. A black solar panel absorbs more energy from sunlight than a white one of the same size. A white panel will reflect more solar radiation. Black surfaces also radiate more energy than white surfaces, but overall a black panel gets warm more quickly and reaches a higher temperature. The higher temperature makes it more efficient at transferring this energy by electricity. Scientists are concerned that the polar ice caps are melting as a result of climate change. Why will it make any difference if the polar ice caps melt? Create an annotated diagram to explain why scientists are concerned.

Forces, energy resources & energy transfer

7.15 Sun as a source of energy

Choose a four-hour period of your life and make a list of all the ways in which you made use of energy (such as going on a bus, jogging, heating water for a shower, using electricity in a washing machine, etc). Discuss the list with your friends. See if you can work out where the energy came from originally and add this to your list. How could a mole that lives underground get energy from the Sun?

Nearly all food chains start with a green plant. Plants capture energy from sunlight during photosynthesis. When we obtain energy by eating food, the energy in it has come from the Sun. Fossil fuels are formed from the remains of animals and plants that lived many millions of years ago. These organisms got their energy from the Sun when they were alive. Many renewable energy sources get their energy from the Sun as well. One example is energy transferred by the wind. The Sun radiates a lot of energy to Earth. This energy is absorbed by the ground and heats the surrounding air. This creates differences in temperature that cause the wind. The wind can turn wind turbines and generate electricity that supplies the National Grid. One exception is geothermal energy, where energy transferred from nuclear reactions deep in the Earth heats water and generates electricity. Draft an outline for a science fiction story in which the Sun is dying and the amount of energy from the Sun is reducing.

7.16 Energy from nuclear fuel

Use textbooks or the internet to research different methods of generating electricity. Talk about what the source of energy is for each method. Produce an annotated diagram for each method to show the essential stages in generating electricity. How can we get energy from the Sun when it is millions of kilometres away?

Most power stations burn fuels to turn water into steam that is used to turn turbines and generate electricity. Nuclear power stations are different. They use nuclear reactions in radioactive materials like uranium or plutonium to generate electricity. Nuclear reactions are not like burning, where chemicals join together to release energy. In a nuclear reaction the structure of some of the atoms is changed and the nuclei of the atoms (made from protons and neutrons) are split into smaller pieces. As they do this they release huge amounts of energy. 1 kg of nuclear fuel can produce the same energy as burning nearly 3 million kg of coal. This energy turns water into steam to drive the turbines. Fossil fuels got their energy from the Sun via plants and animals millions of years ago, but uranium, like lots of the complex elements in the periodic table, was made inside stars at the time of a supernova, long before our Sun was formed. Nuclear power has advantages and disadvantages. Make a table to show what the advantages and disadvantages are.

Forces, energy resources & energy transfer

7.17 Amount of energy from the Sun

Draw a diagram to show energy from the Sun reaching the Earth. Now draw a series of diagrams to represent day and night and the different seasons. Draw another diagram to show clouds covering the Earth's surface. Talk about how these diagrams help you to understand how much energy from the Sun reaches the Earth. Why is energy from the Sun so important to life on Earth? How many reasons can you think of?

The Earth moves in a roughly circular orbit round the Sun. The Sun produces roughly the same amount of energy all the time. This means that the same amount of energy is distributed over the surface of the Earth at all times. Because we get day and night the amount of energy transferred to the surface varies over a 24-hour period in any one place, even though it's constant over the whole Earth's surface. The same thing happens with the seasons, but over a longer period of time. Cloud can make a difference because cloud reflects sunlight back out into space. The more cloud there is, the more sunlight is reflected. If a lot of the Earth is covered in cloud for a long time it reduces the amount of energy transferred to the Earth's surface. Scientists think that one of the reasons that dinosaurs died out during the Cretaceous period was a meteorite impact. Can you explain why this might have caused the dinosaurs to die, and what does it have to do with energy from the Sun?

Forces, energy resources & energy transfer

7.18 Do gliders have energy?

Find some instructions on the internet for how to make a bishop's hat paper glider. Make one and see how well it glides. Talk about how it moves and where the energy needed for movement comes from. How well do your ideas apply to a paper aeroplane and a glider? Why does an aeroplane need an engine if a glider can manage without an engine?

There must be a transfer of energy for the glider to fly. Energy is needed to create enough force to stop it falling straight down to the ground. The shape of its wing creates an upward force (lift) as air flows over it, but it has to keep moving through the air to create this lift. Gliders have to be launched because they have no engine to make them move. Usually a glider is pulled behind another aeroplane and then released. It gains gravitational potential energy from being lifted high up, then gradually falls towards the ground, losing height but keeping its speed up. Energy that has transferred from the Sun can help it regain height. The Sun heats the ground, which heats the air above it and causes the air to rise, creating a thermal (a rising column of air). This thermal creates the lift needed for the glider to gain height. A skilful glider pilot can use thermals to keep pushing the glider upwards and regain any height it loses. Create an energy flow chart to show what happens in terms of energy transfer during the flight of a glider.

Forces, energy resources & energy transfer

7.19 Does energy change form?

Talk together about what you think is happening in terms of energy when you turn on the torch. Where is the energy before you turn on the torch? Where did this energy come from? Where is the energy when you turn the torch off? Use a textbook or the internet to find out more about energy transfer. If energy can't be created or destroyed, why will the torch eventually stop working?

Energy is a difficult concept to explain, so we use models to explain how energy makes things happen. One model is that energy changes from one form (or type) to another. Most scientists think that a better model of energy is that it is stored in different ways and can be transferred from one store to another. The energy does not change – it just makes things happen as it moves around. In this example energy is in a chemical store in the battery. When the torch is switched on the chemicals inside the battery react and create a voltage between the ends of the battery. This voltage pushes an electrical current round the wires and this transfers energy to the lamp. The lamp transfers energy to the surroundings by lighting and heating. Create an energy flow chart to show what happens in terms of energy transfer during some common events in your home (e.g. doing the washing, or watching TV).

7.20 What happens to energy?

Talk together about what you think is happening in terms of energy as the fire burns. Where is the energy before you light the fire? Where did this energy come from? Where is the energy when the fire goes out? Where is energy at the beginning of a food chain, and where is it at the end? If energy can't be created or destroyed, why does the fire eventually go out?

Energy is never created or destroyed. It is just transferred from one place to another. When energy is transferred it enables things to happen. A lot of energy is stored in the wood. As it burns, energy is transferred to the surroundings by heating, lighting and a small amount of sound. The energy hasn't been used up or lost, but as it is transferred to the surroundings it becomes more spread out (dissipated) and it is less able to do work for us. Energy stored in the food does not come from the burning wood. It comes from plants capturing the Sun's energy in photosynthesis, and this energy is transferred to animals in the food chain that eat the plants. Cooking food just makes it tastier and easier to digest. Create an energy flow chart to show what happens when you cook chicken on a barbeque.

Forces, energy resources & energy transfer

Light and shadow

8

8

Light and shadow

8.1 Coloured shadows

Use red, blue and green colour filters and torches to make different colour lights. See what happens if you shine these at the same object from different directions. Notice what happens where the coloured light overlaps. Explore the similarities and differences if you use white instead of coloured lights. What happens if you shine the coloured lights onto different-coloured surfaces?

We normally think of shadows forming when white light coming from one source is blocked by an opaque object or material. No light can get to the area behind the object, so a shadow of the object is formed. If light comes from more than one light source, multiple shadows can be formed but the shadows are partial. You can see this with floodlights on a games pitch. This problem is complicated because the lights are coloured, not white, and come from more than one source. If red and green lights are shining from different directions, the actor has a shadow where the red light is blocked and one where the green light is blocked. The shadow where the red light is blocked is green, because the green light still shines on that part of the stage, and where the green light is blocked the shadow is red. Where primary coloured lights overlap you get the secondary colour. For example, green and red light produces yellow light. Use what you have learnt to write directions for a lighting crew at a concert to get different lighting effects.

143

8.2 Why do roses look red?

Look at a red object through a red colour filter, then through a blue filter. Repeat this with a blue object. Look at different objects through a red and blue filter together. What does this tell you about how light is reflected or absorbed? Predict what you will see if you look at different coloured objects through different filters. If you have access to a spectrometer, use it to check your predictions. Look up how to make a simple spectrometer using a CD.

Sunlight (white light) is made up of all the colours of the spectrum. When you see a rainbow you see white light split into all these colours. When light hits an opaque object it can be reflected or absorbed. White objects absorb very little light and reflect all the colours of the spectrum, so we see them as white. A coloured object reflects some colours of light and absorbs the rest. We only see the light it reflects, so this is the colour the object appears. A red flower reflects red light and absorbs other colours, so we see it as red. In blue light there is no red light to reflect, so the red flower appears black. Can you work out why we get green when we mix yellow and blue (cyan) paint together, but when we mix red and green light we get yellow? Create an advice leaflet for a gardener who wants to know which colours of the spectrum will help green plants to grow well.

8.3 How does light travel at night?

Shine a torch into the sky at night. How far do you think the beam of light goes? Use your torch to signal to a friend at night. How far apart do you think you would have to be before you can't see the light? How far away do you think are the furthest lights you can see? Think about lights that are visible from an aeroplane, or on a satellite image of Earth. On a clear night you will see stars in the sky. How far does light travel from the nearest stars to Earth?

Light travels very quickly, nearly 3 million metres/second. It travels in a straight line unless it is reflected, absorbed or bent by something in its path. At night a light seems brighter than in the daytime because of the contrast between light and darkness. However, it isn't travelling further or faster than during the day. Light can be scattered in different directions by hitting small particles in the air. When you see a bright cloud the light coming through it has been scattered by the water droplets in the cloud. When light travels over a long distance a lot of it may be scattered by particles so we may not see it well. Scientists use light from a laser to measure the distance between the Earth and the Moon. They send a laser pulse of light towards the Moon and measure the time taken for this to be reflected off the Moon and returned to the sender. Create a guide to how lasers are used to measure distances in everyday life. Think up some new ideas if you can.

Light and shadow

8.4 How far does light travel?

Draw a simple diagram of our Solar System. Talk about what to add to your diagram to show how light from the Sun reaches the Earth, and how light from the stars reaches the Earth. When we look at very distant stars we are looking back in time. Can you find out why?

We can see stars in the sky. These stars are in other Solar Systems, so light must be able to travel from stars to our Solar System. Our Sun is a star, so light must be able to leave our Solar System and travel to other Solar Systems as well. As light travels away from our Sun it spreads out in all directions and becomes more diffuse (less concentrated). The further away you get the fainter it appears. Some of the stars are so far away that the light from them is too spread out for us to see with our eyes or with the biggest telescopes. Telescopes that detect microwaves rather than visible light allow us to see further into the Universe. Very distant stars are so far away that the Universe isn't old enough for their light to reach us yet, and this is one reason why the night sky doesn't look really bright. Create a science fiction story about what would happen if light from our Sun got trapped and stopped travelling out of the Solar System.

Light and shadow

8.5 How bright is reflected light?

Light a candle in a dark room. Observe how well you can see things in the room. Now place a large mirror behind the candle. Does it change how bright the light is in the room? Does it make a difference where you are in the room? Try a concave curved mirror and see if that makes any difference. How many different ways can you think of where mirrors are used in everyday life? What extra uses do curved mirrors have?

Safety note: A candle flame is very hot and you could burn yourself or possibly scorch or set fire to something. Make sure you are supervised by an adult, that the candle is secure on a flame-proof surface and cannot fall over. Take care with the lighter or matches you use to light it.

A burning candle produces a fixed amount of light that travels away from the flame in all directions. As it spreads out it is less effective at illuminating things. If you put a mirror close to the candle, the light that hits the mirror is reflected. It is about twice as bright in front of the mirror because of the reflected light (a tiny amount of energy is lost when the light reflects off the mirror). The mirror does not create more light, it simply redirects the light. Behind the mirror there is a shadow because the mirror blocks light in that direction. A concave curved mirror concentrates the reflected light into a smaller area so it can be much brighter there, but there will be a smaller increase in brightness elsewhere in the room. Create some images of new ways to use the reflective properties of mirrors.

Light and shadow

8.6 The angle of reflected light

Shine a torch onto a mirror from different angles in a darkened room, and see what happens. Turn the mirror at different angles. Look for any patterns in the way the light reflects from the mirror. Repeat with a piece of white paper or plastic. Make a periscope and draw ray diagrams to explain how it works.

Light normally travels in a straight line in air. When it hits something it is either reflected, refracted or absorbed. Usually light that is reflected bounces off the surface at any angle (it is scattered) because the surface is rough. Even if it doesn't feel rough, it can be rough at a microscopic level. Mirrors reflect nearly all the light that falls on them in an unusual way. The light is reflected at the same angle as the angle that it hits the mirror. Also the light rays that hit a mirror don't get mixed up. The mirror reflects the light and keeps the rays in the same order so we see a clear image of the object the light came from. Any very smooth polished surface can act as a mirror. The smoother the mirror, the better the reflections are and the better the image. Metals, or glass coated with a metal, work especially well. What do you think the first mirrors were made from? Use what you have learnt to explain how Archimedes' idea of a 'heat ray' might have been used to attack enemy ships during the Siege of Syracuse.

Light and shadow

8.7 Real and apparent depth

Put a modelling clay fish at the bottom of a tank of water. Try to spear the fish with a pencil. Talk about where you have to aim to hit the fish. Put your pencil diagonally in the water, half in and half out, and see how it looks. Which way does it appear to bend? An archer fish catches its prey by shooting a jet of water at an insect from below the surface of the water. What problems does the archer fish have to overcome to do this successfully?

As light goes from water into air it bends. This is called refraction. It happens when light hits water at an angle because light travels more slowly in water than in air. It's a bit like pushing a trolley with a sticking wheel that pulls the trolley round as you move forward. When this light reaches our eyes the brain interprets what it sees as though the light is travelling in a straight line. This causes the water to appear shallower than it really is, and objects like fish to seem higher in the water than they really are. Light bends in the opposite direction when it travels from water to air. Different substances bend light by different amounts. The speed the water is flowing at doesn't make any difference to how much light bends. Different wavelengths of light bend by different amounts too, which is how a prism splits white light into different colours. Create some images to show how refraction sometimes lets us see mirages on a very hot day.

8.8 What do lenses do?

Make a thin beam of light by shining a torch through a thin slit in a piece of black card. In a darkened room, shine the thin beam of light through different things, such as a flat piece of glass, a clear glass bottle, a clear glass bottle full of water, a magnifying glass and so on. Talk about what seems to be happening to the beam of light. Use the internet to find a video of what happens when light is shone through a lens. What do you think will happen if you shine a beam of light through a concave lens (one that is thick at the edges and thin in the middle)?

When light hits a transparent substance like glass, some of it gets reflected and some passes through the glass. Light travels at different speeds in glass and in air. This means that as the light goes from air into glass, it bends. This is called refraction. Different materials bend the light by different amounts. A magnifying glass is a convex lens, thick in the middle and thinner at the edges. All the light passing through it bends towards one point. The combination of refraction of the light and the curve of the lens focuses the light. You can show how this happens using ray diagrams. Create an information leaflet to help people understand how refraction at the cornea and lens in the eye enable us to see clearly.

Light and shadow

8.9 Which lens corrects poor eyesight?

In a darkened room, shine a thin beam of light through different types of lenses. Talk about what happens to the light with each type of lens and draw diagrams to show what is happening. Use books or the internet to check what kind of lenses can correct visual defects. Why do convex lenses and concave mirrors focus light, but concave lenses and convex mirrors don't?

To focus light into a small spot you need a convex lens, thick in the middle and thin at the edges. Long-sighted people have a lens in their eye that is not strong enough to focus the light on the retina. A convex lens in their spectacles bends the light rays inwards, ready for the lens in the eye to bend it more so that it is in focus. Short-sighted people have a lens in their eye that bends the light too much, so that it is out of focus when it reaches the retina. They need concave lenses in their spectacles to bend the light rays apart a little, so the lens in the eye focuses it on the retina. You could light a fire with spectacles for a long-sighted person but not for a short-sighted person. The convex lens focuses infrared radiation as well as visible light, and the infrared radiation makes things hot and can start a fire. Create a poster that an optician could use to explain to customers how spectacles help to correct short or long sight.

8.10 How fast does light travel?

You won't be able to measure the speed of light, and you won't be able to measure how far away the stars are. How do you think scientists manage to measure these things? Talk about your ideas, then use a book or the internet to find out whether your ideas are correct. Discuss what you know about refraction and why it happens. Why do you think that thin strands of glass (optical fibre cables) are used for telecommunications?

The speed of light in a vacuum (empty space) is just under 300 000 000 metres every second (m/s). The stars in the sky are a huge distance from Earth, so it takes light over 4 years to reach us from the nearest star, called Proxima Centauri. Light from the furthest objects we know about in the universe has taken about 13 billion years to get to us. That's 13 000 000 000 years. The speed of light in air is slightly slower, but only by about 0.03%, so it is very close to the speed of light in a vacuum. Light travels more slowly in transparent objects – about 25% slower in water and about 33% slower in some types of glass. Create an annotated drawing to show why light appears to bend as it moves from air into water or glass.

8.11 What is electromagnetic radiation?

Find a picture of the electromagnetic spectrum. Discuss what you know about the parts that you recognise. Do some research to find out exactly what the spectrum is. Talk about what life would be like if we didn't know how to use electromagnetic radiation. Use the internet to find out why some of the radiation that we can't see helps us to observe the Universe and find out more about it.

Electromagnetic radiation can be thought of as a wave made from electric and magnetic fields that travel at the speed of light. It includes a wide spectrum from radio waves to gamma rays, arranged in order of their wavelength. It is all the same type of radiation, even though the wavelength varies. We can only see a small part of the electromagnetic spectrum, called visible light. Radio waves have the longest wavelength, then, in order, microwaves, infrared and visible light. After visible light comes ultraviolet, x-rays and finally gamma rays. Infrared radiation is emitted by hot objects; this is what makes us feel warm in the sunshine or standing next to a barbeque. Ultraviolet radiation has a much shorter wavelength and is the radiation that causes sunburn when our skin is exposed to it. Create a chart to show the different parts of the spectrum and how each type of radiation can be used.

8.12 Is all radiation dangerous?

Look at a diagram of the electromagnetic spectrum. Talk about what property makes the types of radiation different from each other. See if you can invent a way to remember the order of the electromagnetic spectrum. Find out which types of radiation are dangerous and how we can avoid being harmed by radiation. Talk about what life would be like if we didn't know how to use electromagnetic radiation.

Radiation is all around us. The light entering your eye is radiation. Visible light is a small part of the electromagnetic spectrum that stretches from radio waves through to gamma rays. Some types of radiation are harmful because they transfer energy to our cells. However every type of radiation can also be useful. For example, too many gamma rays or X-rays can destroy cells or change their DNA to make them cancerous. But X-rays help us see inside the body, and both of these types of radiation are used to kill cancer cells. Some types of microwaves can cause water to heat up, and since our cells are full of water they can harm us. Other sorts of microwaves carry mobile phone signals and do very little harm. Too much ultraviolet radiation can give you sunburn or cause skin cancers, but our skin needs ultraviolet radiation to make vitamin D. It is important to avoid exposure to too much of the wrong sorts of radiation. Create a chart to show the risks and benefits of radiation for parents who are worried about radiation.

Sound

9

6

9.1 Vibrating strings

Investigate sounds using a stringed instrument, like a guitar or violin. Alternatively, experiment with elastic bands, stretched over an open box to help you hear the sounds better. Try different thicknesses of elastic bands and plucking the elastic band in different ways. How do these change the sound? Apart from how loud the sound is, what other ways are there of describing a sound? How can you measure these?

Sound is a vibration that travels through the air or some other medium. We detect sound as it makes our eardrums vibrate. The bigger the vibration, the bigger the amplitude of the sound wave and the louder the sound seems to be. To get a guitar string to vibrate more you have to pluck it harder. It is easier to do this near the middle of the string rather than at one end. Plucking the string harder does not change how high the note is. Plucking it harder transfers more energy to the string, so the note is louder and lasts longer. To get a louder sound in a wind instrument (e.g. saxophone) or a percussion instrument (e.g. cymbal) you have to transfer more energy by blowing or hitting it harder. It isn't always easy to tell how loud a sound is because human ears are more sensitive to medium-pitched sounds than very low and very high-pitched sounds. What would you advise musicians to do if they want a loud note that only lasts a short amount of time? Is it the same for every instrument?

9.2 Changing the length of a string

Use a stringed instrument, such as a guitar or violin, to investigate the effect of changing the length of string. Alternatively, experiment with elastic bands, stretched over an open box to help you hear the sounds better. Find out how the length of the elastic band changes the sound. Find out how the amount the elastic band is stretched changes the sound. Talk about how you could measure how loud the sounds are and how far or how fast they travel. Is there a limit to how high or low a sound you can make using a stretched elastic band or string?

Instruments with strings make sounds when the string vibrates and the energy of this vibration is transferred to our ears by sound waves. Our ears can detect the frequency of the sound waves – that is, how many sound waves there are per second. If the string vibrates more quickly then there are more sound waves per second. When the frequency is higher, the pitch of the sound is higher. The shorter a string is, the faster it vibrates and the higher the pitch of the sound. Changing the length of the string does not affect how loud the sound is, the distance that sound waves travel or the speed that they travel. In wind instruments the pitch is altered by changing the length of a column of air that is vibrating. Create a set of annotated drawings to help someone to understand sound waves and pitch.

9.3 Reflecting sounds

Go into different spaces such as a gym, a classroom or hall. Clap your hands and see what happens. Do you hear an echo? What do you think an echo is and why do you think it happens? Use a datalogger to record some sounds and investigate whether a mirror makes the sound louder. Try different kinds of mirrors. Find out whether it makes a difference if the mirror is flat or curved. Does it matter which way the mirror is curved? Does the size of the mirror make a difference? What happens if you try other surfaces?

We hear the bell because it vibrates and sends vibrations, known as sound waves, through the air. The sound waves travel in all directions away from the vibrating object. Some of the sound from the bell can be reflected by smooth hard surfaces like a mirror, a wall or a table. The mirror doesn't create any more sound. However, if sound is reflected then there are extra vibrations reflected in that direction, so the bell seems louder. A concave dish-shaped surface can concentrate sound in one direction better than a flat surface, so the reflected sound seems louder than sound reflected off a flat surface. Exactly how much louder depends on the size and curvature of the mirror. A large curved mirror can make the sound seem a lot louder. Why do you think radio telescopes are the shape that they are? How are they different from optical telescopes?

9.4 What can block sound waves?

Bang a drum or play some music in a room and shut the door. Find out how far away from the closed door someone has to go until they can't hear it. Find out whether it makes a difference if they go round a corner, or if the door is open. Get them to press their ear to the door, or put their ear to a glass held against the door. Does this make a difference to what they hear? Talk about what you think is happening. How do you think earplugs work?

When we bang a drum we cause the skin of the drum to vibrate. The vibrating drum skin causes the particles in the air to vibrate and transmit sound waves in every direction. When the sound waves hit a door they make some of the particles in the door vibrate as well. Some of these vibrations are passed on to the air on the other side of the door, so we can hear them when the door is closed. Only some of the sound reaches the other side of the door, so the sound is quieter. Some of the sound is reflected back into the room by the door and other hard surfaces, and some of its energy makes the room slightly warmer, so we can't hear that part. What advice would you give to someone who wants to prevent sounds coming through the wall of their house, and why?

9.5 Does sound travel through water?

Talk about what happens when you swim under water. Can you hear sounds that people make under the water? Can you hear sounds that people make out of the water? Investigate sounds under water using a sound probe or microphone in a plastic bag (so the water won't damage it). Put your ear against a tank of water and make sounds in the water. What do you hear? Whales and some other animals make sounds under water. Listen to whale songs on the internet. Why do you think whales sing? Do you think whales have ears?

Sound is caused by vibrations that travel through things. Vibrations are passed from particle to particle, so sound can travel through anything where the particles are close enough together to pass on vibrations. Air particles are close enough to do this. Particles in a liquid or solid are closer together, so they pass on vibrations more easily. When a sound in the air reaches water, it is not easy for the vibrating air particles to transfer energy to the water particles. The sound doesn't transfer easily from air to water, so it is harder for the sound to reach the fish in the water. However, sound travels so well in water that whales can communicate over thousands of kilometres using sound. Fish have internal ears and they also detect vibrations in the water using a line of sensors along their sides called the lateral line. Draw a diagram to show how you think having a lateral line helps a fish to survive.

9.6 What does sound travel through?

Find a clock with a loud tick. Get some different materials at least one metre long (e.g. wood, plastic, metal) and put the clock against each material. Now put your ear against the other end of each material. How well can you hear the sound through the material? How does it compare with listening to the sound through the air? Fill a long balloon or plastic bag with water and listen to the sound again. Is there any difference in what you hear when the sound travels through different substances?

Sound travels away from a source by making the particles next to it vibrate. These particles pass on the vibrations to the particles next to them, and this next set of particles pass on the vibrations, and so on. The closer together the particles are, the better the sound travels. The particles in gases are spread out and not touching each other, so sounds travel slowest in gases. Sounds travel fastest in solids and nearly as fast in liquids. Most of the sounds we hear have travelled through air. Sounds that travel to us through solids or liquids can sound different. This is because different frequencies of sound travel more or less easily in solids and liquids, so the quality of the sound changes. Musicians such as Michel Redolfi play music concerts underwater. Find out more about this music and draw a picture of what you think an underwater concert will look like.

Sound

9.7 Can sound travel round corners?

With a friend, stand on opposite sides of a wall. Play a radio on one side of the wall and see if you can hear it on the other side and how loud the sound is. A datalogger will make this more accurate. Make a barrier with a large book, or some other object. Use a datalogger to measure whether the volume of the sound from the radio changes as you move the sensor behind the object. Discuss what this tells you about the way that sound travels. Make some ripples in water and see if they go round corners or objects. How might watching ripples help you to learn about sound travelling?

Sound waves travel in all directions away from the vibrating object that is making the sound. As they travel further the sound seems quieter because the energy transferred by the wave has spread out more. Sound waves can be reflected by hard surfaces but they can also go around things. This bending is known as diffraction. When this happens the sound usually gets quieter. The more reflections and diffractions a sound makes on its journey to your ears, the quieter it gets. With enough diffractions and reflections, eventually a sound might get too quiet for you to hear. Prepare an advice sheet for a designer to explain how sound reflection and diffraction are important when designing a music venue with good acoustics.

9.8 Can you hear an earthquake?

Explore how well vibrations pass through solid materials by putting your ear to a long piece of wood or metal pipe and tapping the other end gently. Talk about what you think is the biggest distance a vibration could travel through the Earth. Use books or the internet to find out about the frequency of vibration of earthquakes. Find out about the two types of waves that are made during an earthquake and how they are different. How do these waves fit with the range of human hearing?

The vibrations made by an earthquake are very low frequency. The frequency of these vibrations is normally too low to hear, but we can feel them in our bodies. Some people claim to hear a boom from an earthquake. This might be because some earthquakes are shallower than others, and this causes higher-frequency vibrations. The movements in an earthquake make other things around us vibrate (which is why buildings get damaged), and we may hear these vibrations. Some of the Earth's vibrations are passed to the air and travel as a low-frequency sound wave that we might hear. Vibrations travel much further and faster through the Earth (which is mostly solids and liquids) than through the air. A seismometer is used to measure the magnitude of an earthquake. Using this information about earthquakes, sketch a simple design for how you think a seismometer might work.

9.9 How does double glazing work?

Use a datalogger to measure how well sound travels through one, two, or three layers of glass, and layers of glass with an air gap between them. Find out more about double glazing on the internet. Sometimes most of the air is removed from between the two panes of glass. What difference do you think this will make to the amount of sound that you hear?

When sound waves hit a piece of glass they transfer energy and make it vibrate. Some of the sound waves are reflected off the glass. Some of the sound waves makes the glass slightly warmer. The rest of the vibration travels through the glass and makes the air on the other side vibrate. In double glazing the sound has to do this twice, so more energy is reflected or is transferred into the glass to make it slightly warmer. The trapped air and the layer of glass both act as sound insulators. Triple glazing, or removing the air between the panes of glass, are even better at keeping the sound out. A thicker layer of glass would not be as efficient as double glazing. Reflective glass still allows sound to pass through. Even with double-glazed windows some of the sound may still pass through the frame around the glass. Draw a double-glazed window, and use coloured arrows to show how energy is transferred when a sound wave hits the window.

9.10 Thermal and sound insulation

Get hold of some ear muffs. Investigate whether they keep your ears warm and whether you can hear properly wearing them. Use sound and temperature probes to compare the insulation properties of different materials. Use a simple low-voltage circuit to see if the materials conduct electricity. Is there any pattern in the insulating properties of different materials? Are there any exceptions to the pattern? What about the insulating properties of a vacuum.

Safety note: some insulating materials, such as loft insulation, may not be safe to use. It's important to check first.

Air is a good thermal insulator. Most thermal insulators work by trapping lots of air in pockets, bubbles or layers. This is how fur and wool keep us warm. A sound insulator stops sound waves travelling through it because it absorbs or reflects the vibrations of sound waves. Soft or rough materials tend to absorb sound vibrations, and so do materials with lots of trapped air (just like double glazing does). Many thermal insulators are therefore sound insulators too. However some high-density materials (such as wood) can be thermal insulators but transmit sound very well. Good electrical insulators won't let electricity pass through them because of the way the particles in the material behave. Materials that are good sound insulators are often electrical insulators but not always. Steel wool can be a good sound insulator but conducts electricity. A vacuum prevents most types of energy transfer, but does allow electromagnetic radiation to be transmitted. What practical advice would you give to someone who wants to make a soundproof recording studio and why?

166

9.11 The speed of light and sound

Think about examples of when you see something before you hear it, such as thunder and lightning. Talk about when this happens and whether it is always that way round. Use books or the internet to find out more about how light and sound travel and how fast they travel. Imagine there is a gigantic explosion on the Moon. Would it be possible to see and hear the explosion? Would the infrared radiation released make you feel warmer?

Sound travels as a wave, through vibrations that are passed on from one air particle to another. It can't travel through a vacuum because there are no particles to pass on the vibrations. Light is more complicated. It is a form of electromagnetic radiation that travels in tiny units called photons. In some ways these photons act like waves, and in other ways like very fast particles. Light can travel through a vacuum and can also travel through air. In air, sound travels at about 1 km in 3 seconds. Light travels at the fastest speed possible, about 300 000 km/sec (about 300 000 000 m/sec), which is nearly a million times faster than sound. You always see the firework before you hear it because of the difference in speed between sound and light. It doesn't make any difference whether it's windy or how big the firework is. Write an explanation of how to calculate how far away a storm is by counting the time between the thunder and the lightning.

9.12 Reflection and refraction

Talk about the meaning of reflection and refraction. Do an internet search to check your ideas. Test your understanding by explaining to each other why a spoon looks bent when you lower it into a glass of water, and what happens to light when you shine it through different-shaped blocks of transparent material. Use mirrors and a datalogger to explore your ideas about reflection of sound. Refraction of sound is complicated to investigate, but you can find animations of this on the internet. What can you find out about mirages and what causes them, and how is this connected to reflection and refraction?

As light moves from water into air, it bends because of the different speeds that light travels through air and through water. This is called refraction. The amount that light bends can be predicted, and ray diagrams can illustrate why the light bending makes a spoon look broken. Light is also reflected, and we see things when light is reflected from objects into our eyes. Sound can be reflected and refracted too. If you stand in front of a tall building and make a loud noise, the echo you hear is a reflection. The speed of sound in air depends on the temperature, and refraction usually happens when sound waves travel at different speeds through air at different temperatures. Create an image bank of everyday situations where reflection and refraction of sound and light occur, with captions to indicate the effect of reflection and refraction.

9.13 Is ultrasound a sound?

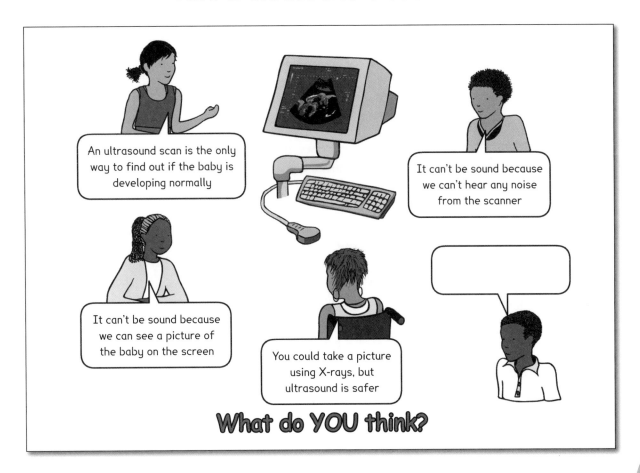

Find some examples of ultrasound pictures on the internet. Talk about what the word 'ultra' means, and what the difference is between sound and ultrasound. Look for pictures of different sorts of bats and check what their ears look like. Why do you think they are like that?

Our ears detect sound waves, including how frequently the sound waves arrive at our ears. When there are more sound waves per second, the pitch of the sound is higher. We can only hear sounds up to a frequency of about 20 000 sound waves a second (Hertz or Hz), and less than this as we get older. Frequencies higher than this are still sounds but we cannot hear them. We call them ultrasound. Ultrasound is used to detect things inside the body by projecting ultrasound waves into the body and collecting reflections off the internal organs. A transducer turns the sounds into an image we can see on a screen. X-rays also allow us to detect internal organs, but they are more damaging to the body than ultrasound. Reflected ultrasound is also used by many bats to detect objects, because they have very poor eyesight and usually fly at night. They make very high-frequency clicks and squeaks and listen to reflections from objects, including reflections from the prey they are hunting. Reflected sound (SONAR) is used to detect fish, submarines and other objects under water. Sketch a diagram to show how you think this might work.

169

9.14 Sounds that we can't hear

Have you ever used a dog whistle? If you can get hold of one, try one to check whether you can hear it. There are videos on the internet you can listen to. Dog whistles often have a screw to adjust the pitch. Talk about why you think manufacturers make them like this. Check your answer on the internet, or with a dog owner.

The number of sound waves each second is known as the frequency, measured in Hertz (Hz). Human beings can't hear sounds above about 20 000 Hz. High-pitched sounds have a high frequency. Dogs can hear much higher-pitched sounds than humans, up to about 60 000 Hz depending on the type and age of the dog. Dog whistles produce a very high-pitched sound that we can't hear but dogs can. Sounds usually travel at the same speed in air, about 340 metres/second. The length of each sound wave, or wavelength, changes with the frequency. The higher the frequency, the shorter the wavelength. Three properties of a wave – its speed, wavelength and frequency – are linked together by a mathematical formula that states Speed = Frequency x Wavelength. This is known as the wave equation. Choose some other animals and identify the frequency ranges they can hear. Create a powerpoint presentation, or some other visual display, to show how hearing these frequencies might help them to survive.

170

9.15 The Doppler effect

Look up the Doppler effect on the internet and watch a demonstration video. Talk about when you hear this effect in everyday life. Does how fast the sound source is travelling make a difference? Can you go fast enough on a bicycle to be able to hear the Doppler effect?

The frequency of a sound is the number of waves per second that the sound source makes. A high-frequency sound has a high pitch. If an object moves towards you, making a sound wave, each peak of the wave is generated slightly closer to you than the last peak. This makes the sound waves arrive slightly earlier, the time between the wave peaks is reduced and the frequency is slightly higher than it would be for a stationary object. The sound wave gets a bit squashed up. When the object goes away from you, the sound wave gets a bit stretched out and the frequency gets less because each peak is generated a little bit further away from you. As the object passes you, the sound quickly changes in frequency from higher to lower. Light also travels in waves, so it does the same thing. Astronomers use this to calculate how fast stars or galaxies are approaching or moving away from Earth. This change in the frequency of a wave is called the Doppler effect. Draw a diagram to explain how the Doppler effect could be used in a speed camera to identify speeding motorists.

9.16 Does sound exist in a vacuum?

Look up a definition of sound. Talk about whether the sound depends on somebody being there to hear it. Find out about how sounds travel in air. Use the internet to find video clips of astronauts on the Moon or in space. Talk about how astronauts communicate with each other. How much noise is there on the Moon or in space? If there is less air at the top of Mount Everest than at sea level, will that affect what we hear?

Sound waves are vibrations carried from a source to our ears. Usually the sound waves are carried through the air. Objects that make sounds are vibrating, like the speaker on a TV or radio. The vibration causes air particles to vibrate in the layer of air directly touching the source. This layer of vibrating particles passes the vibration on to the next set of particles. This process carries on as the vibration passes through the air. The sound waves are still there even if there is nothing to detect them, so sound can exist even when nobody is there to hear it. Sound cannot travel through a vacuum because there are no particles to pass the vibrations on. There is a vacuum in outer space so sounds can't travel. Do a short review of the science in extracts from films that are set in outer space. Do film-makers get the science of sound right? For example, how much noise is there in a space battle scene?

Sound

Earth, space and gravity

10

173

10

Earth, space and gravity

10.1 Do stars make their own light?

Talk about when you see stars best and whether they seem brighter in the countryside or in a town. Find out which of the stars we see are really distant galaxies. Make a list of information about the Sun (our star). You could include information about its size, temperature, age and what it is made from. If it creates its own light, where do you think the energy comes from to generate so much light?

The stars we see at night are like our Sun, but much further away. Some are very large and others smaller, some are very hot and others less hot. Our Sun is an average size and temperature for a star. Just like our Sun, stars make light because they are made from hydrogen, which can release energy by nuclear fusion. The surface of some stars can be as hot as 50 000°C, and gases at that temperature produce a lot of light. The stars are there all the time, during the day and at night. We only see the other stars at night because the Earth is close to the Sun, so the Sun's light is much brighter than light from other stars. Some of the things that look like single stars are actually huge clusters of stars, known as galaxies, but so far away that we see them as a single point of light. Create a simple comparison table to show the difference between light from the Moon, the Sun, the stars and galaxies.

Earth, space and gravity

10.2 Do planets create their own light?

Share what you know about where and how light is produced. Find out when Venus is visible in the sky and talk about why you think it isn't visible all of the time. Draw a model of the solar system on a large sheet of paper and use a highlighter to indicate where light is produced and reflected. Use your model to talk about how we can see the Moon, the planets, the Sun and the stars. Why do stars appear to twinkle but planets don't?

Planets, moons and asteroids do not make their own light. We see them because they reflect light from the Sun. Venus has a dense atmosphere, made up of mainly carbon dioxide and nitrogen, with clouds of sulfuric acid. The clouds reflect most of the sunlight, which is why Venus looks so bright in the sky. Venus is a yellowy-white colour when viewed from Earth. Venus is only visible in the early morning or early evening, and from Earth it is the third brightest thing you can see, after the Sun and Moon. With a telescope it is clear that Venus has phases, just like the Moon does, depending on its position relative to the Sun and Earth. Create an annotated drawing to show why the Moon appears to be so much brighter than Venus in the night sky.

Earth, space and gravity

10.3 What causes a lunar eclipse?

Set up a model using balls or fruit of different sizes to represent the Earth, Sun and Moon. Model what happens when the Earth orbits the Sun and the Moon orbits the Earth. Talk about where they have to be for a solar eclipse to happen and where they have to be for a lunar eclipse. Why doesn't the Moon usually go completely dark during a lunar eclipse?

The Earth travels around the Sun in a nearly circular path called an orbit. As it does this, the Moon orbits the Earth. We see the Moon because it reflects light from the Sun. We see different amounts of the illuminated part of the Moon at different times, so the shape of the Moon appears to change. A lunar eclipse is different from this. Sometimes the Earth gets in the way of light from the Sun and stops it reaching the Moon. The Earth casts a shadow on the Moon's surface. Because of the speed the Earth and Moon are travelling, the shadow passes over the Moon quite quickly. If the Earth, Sun and Moon line up exactly we get a total lunar eclipse, where the Moon is completely in the shadow of the Earth for a short time. This is quite rare. Draw an annotated diagram to show why we don't get a lunar eclipse every month.

10.4 What makes planets orbit the Sun?

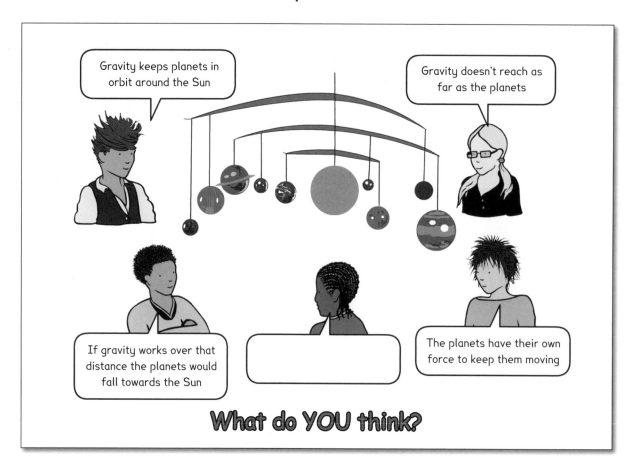

Hold a piece of string, and tie a polystyrene or foam ball onto the other end. Whirl it round so that the ball moves in a circle. Warn people that you are letting go, then let go of the string. Talk about what happens and why it doesn't happen while you hold the string. Try to explain what is happening in terms of forces. How does what happens to the ball help you to understand why the planets go round the Sun roughly in a circle, instead of flying off at an angle? How is gravity connected to the way stars and planets form?

Gravity is a force that makes objects attract each other. It is caused by the combined mass of the objects, so it is tiny for small objects, but very strong for large objects like the Sun. It is strong enough to hold you down on the Earth's surface. Gravity attracts things no matter how far away they are, although it gets much weaker as the distance increases. Gravity is the force that keeps the planets travelling in an orbit round the Sun. Without gravity they would continue to move in a straight line in space. Because of the speed the planets travel, they can be pulled by gravity and not get closer to the Sun. The gravitational force is enough to make them travel in an orbit, but not enough to pull them closer. Find out about 'Newton's cannonball', and write an explanation of this in your own words.

Earth, space and gravity

10.5 Is there gravity on the Moon?

Find a video clip of astronauts on the Moon. Watch how they walk and move about. Watch when they jump, and notice how far they jump. How does this compare with how far you can jump here on the Earth? What does this tell you about gravity on the Moon? Some people think that the Apollo astronauts would have floated away from the Moon if they weren't wearing heavy boots. What do you think?

Neil Armstrong and Buzz Aldrin were the first people to walk on the Moon. Without gravity they would not have been able to do this. Without gravity it would be difficult to land on the Moon and if you tried to take a step you would drift off into space. Gravity is needed to pull you down so you can stand on the ground and take some steps. Gravity on the Moon is about one sixth of gravity on the Earth, so everything weighs much less on the Moon and people can jump further. The Earth's atmosphere is held in place by gravity. The Moon's gravity is not strong enough to hold on to gases, so they just drift away into space, and therefore the Moon has no atmosphere. How would you explain to a young person why a rock and a feather fall differently on the Moon compared to on Earth?

10.6 Daylength at the equator

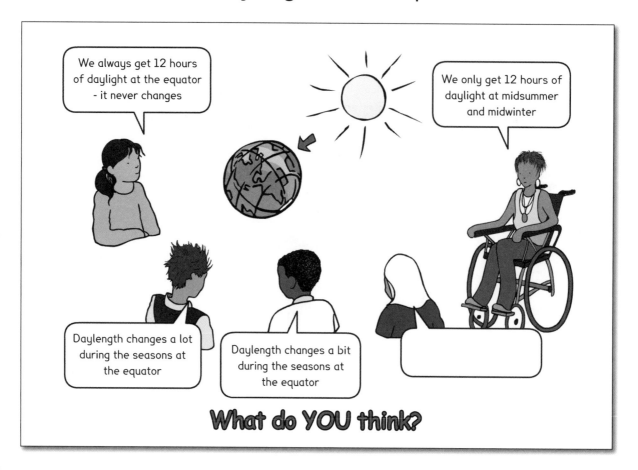

The simplest way to find out about cars getting hotter in the Sun is to make a model. You can do this by getting two similar boxes and painting them black or white, then leaving them in the sunshine for a while. You can compare the temperatures in the two boxes by using a thermometer or temperature sensor inside each box. Does the colour make a difference to the temperature? What happens if you test other colours (green, red, blue, etc.) in the same way?

The equator is the imaginary line that goes round the middle of the Earth and divides the Northern Hemisphere from the Southern Hemisphere. The Earth is tilted to one side by about 23° as it spins. In summer in the Northern Hemisphere the Earth is tilted so the Northern Hemisphere faces more towards the Sun. This means more of it is lit up by the Sun and less is in shadow, so days are longer and nights are shorter. At the equator, the path the Sun appears to take across the sky is slightly to the north during the northern summer, and slightly to the south in the southern summer. At the spring and autumn equinox the Sun is directly overhead at midday. However daylength is always about 12 hours at the equator. Because the Sun appears as a large object in the sky (not as a point source of light) and because the light from the Sun is refracted by the atmosphere, actual daylength at the equator is about 12 hours 7 minutes. Find a way to present information to explain where in the world it can be daylight all the time and where it can be night all the time at certain times of year.

10.7 Why is it hotter in the summer?

Make a model to explore what happens to the Sun and the Earth in summer and winter. Here are some questions to think about with your model. Does everywhere on Earth get summer and winter at the same time? Does the Earth's tilt make any difference? How do daylength and the position of the Sun in the sky change during the year? Does the amount of energy coming from the Sun change during the year? Is it cold all year round in some places? Why do you think it is hot all year round in countries near the equator?

The increased temperature in summer cannot be caused by the Sun getting closer or producing more energy. If this is the reason the whole Earth would have summer at the same time, and we don't. The Earth goes round the Sun in a nearly circular orbit. The Earth does not spin upright, it is tilted to one side by about 23°. When it is summer in the Northern Hemisphere, the Earth is tilted with the Northern Hemisphere facing more towards the Sun, so the sunlight hits the surface at a steeper angle and the solar radiation is more concentrated. The tilt also means that daylength is longer, so the air, water, soil and buildings have longer to absorb energy from the sunlight, which makes the whole environment warmer. Use your model to produce a presentation to explain this to other people.

Earth, space and gravity

10.8 Sundial

Draw the shadows that the Sun makes as it appears to move across the sky during the day. Mark on your drawing the directions of N, S, E and W. Compare the shadow pattern with the hours on a sundial. Think about which way the Sun appears to move in the sky in the Northern and the Southern Hemisphere. Draw a diagram of the Sun, the Earth and your sundial in different positions on the Earth's surface to help you. What will change on your sundial? Find pictures of sundials on the internet to check your answer. Can you draw a diagram to show why the length of the shadow changes during the day?

The apparent movement of the Sun across the sky depends on where you are. If the Sun is to the south of you during the day then it appears to move clockwise across the sky, from east, through south to west. If the Sun is to the north of you during the day then it appears to move anticlockwise across the sky, from east, through north to west. Shadows on the Earth's surface or on a sundial follow the same pattern as the apparent movement of the Sun, so this can be clockwise or anticlockwise, depending on where it is on the Earth's surface. The order of the numbers on the sundial needs to go clockwise in the Northern Hemisphere and anticlockwise in the Southern Hemisphere. Which way will the numbers go in a sundial you could use at the equator?

Earth, space and gravity

10.9 Do stars move?

Look at the stars at night and note the position of a familiar group of stars against something that isn't moving. Look at them again after a while and see if they have moved. If they do appear to move, how quickly do they move? Compare this with how quickly the Sun and the Moon appear to move across the sky. Do they all move in the same direction? Will it be the same in the Northern and Southern Hemispheres?

The Earth spins as it orbits the Sun, and this makes it look as if the Sun, Moon and stars are travelling across the sky. It takes 24 hours for the Earth to do one rotation, so they take 24 hours to appear to move round the Earth and return to their original position. They appear to move slowly from east to west. In the Northern Hemisphere the Pole Star (North Star) doesn't appear to move much. It is nearly in line with the north end of the Earth's axis, so the apparent movement is very small. There isn't a bright star over the south end of the axis, so there is no southern pole star. The Southern Cross points towards where a southern pole star would be. The Moon also orbits the Earth, and this makes it seem like the Moon is moving slightly more slowly than the stars behind it. How would you explain why prominent stars like the North Star and Southern Cross were important for sailors in the past.

Earth, space and gravity

10.10 What if the Earth wasn't tilted?

Find out what angle the Earth is tilted at. Make a model to explore what difference it would make if the Earth wasn't tilted, or if the tilt was 90°. Talk about what difference it would make to daylength, to seasons and to temperature on different parts of the Earth. If you could choose the angle that the Earth is tilted at, what angle would you choose and why?

If the Earth wasn't tilted there would be no seasons. The changes we associate with seasons, like daylength changing, plants flowering, animals producing young and the weather changing, would not happen. However it wouldn't be harder to survive without any seasons. If the tilt was permanently 90°, things would be very different. Some parts of the Earth would face the Sun constantly and would be extremely hot. Other parts of the Earth would be constantly cold, like the coldest parts of the Antarctic in the winter. This would only slowly change as the Earth orbits the Sun, with the hot parts becoming cold and the cold parts becoming hot. Animals and plants would evolve very differently in these very different environments. Create a comparison table to show what the main effects would be for different angles that the Earth might be tilted, such as 0°, 23°, 45° and 90°. What difference would it make to the animals and plants living on Earth?

184

10.11 Is it always cold in space?

Find out how the temperature changes with altitude on Earth, and what the temperature is outside the Earth's atmosphere. Use the internet to find out what the temperature is on each of the planets in our solar system. Talk about whether there is any connection between the surface temperature of the planet and the distance from the Sun, and whether any other factors seem to be important. How does learning about greenhouses help us to work out why Venus, not Mercury, is the hottest planet in the solar system?

The main source of energy in space is stars like our Sun. The nearer a star you are, the hotter it is. A spacecraft in orbit round the Earth gets hot in the sunlight (up to 135°C) and cold in the shadow (as low as -150°C). The temperature on a planet's surface is affected by several factors including the temperature of the planet's core (nuclear reactions can heat up the core of a planet), its atmosphere (the presence of an atmosphere increases the temperature on the surface) and how far it is from the Sun (the closer to the Sun, the higher the temperature). The atmosphere on Venus keeps the surface temperature at about 400°C. Beyond our Solar System temperatures can drop to about -270°C. Create a chart to show the temperature on the surface of the planets in our Solar System. For each planet in your chart, include a paragraph to explain why it is that temperature.

10.12 The Big Bang

Use reference sources to find out more about the origin of the Universe. Use more than one source to get a balance of views. Talk about the different theories that might explain the origin of the Universe. How do the different theories explain the stages in the life of a star?

The Big Bang theory is accepted by most scientists. It states that all the matter in the Universe was created in an event about 14 billion years ago. It suggests that the actual space the universe exists in was created along with the Universe, and that space has been expanding ever since. Stars began to form from clouds of gas pulled together by gravity. This happened less than a billion years after the Big Bang and stars are still being formed today. They produce energy by nuclear fusion for billions of years, and then either slowly cool and become less active, or sometimes they explode in a spectacular supernova. The material from exploding stars gets recycled and forms new stars and planets. All the complex elements present on Earth were formed in supernovae billions of years ago. We don't know if the expanding Universe will stop expanding and then get pulled back together by gravity. If it does it is possible there will be another Big Bang and another universe, but nobody knows. Create a timeline to show how the Universe has changed from its beginning to the present day.

Earth, space and gravity

10.13 Do things get lighter with height?

Talk about what you know about astronauts in the International Space Station. Do they seem lighter or heavier? What does this suggest about whether gravity changes as you go further away from the Earth? Discuss what this suggests about gravity and a hot air balloon. Hot air balloons burn propane to get off the ground. Does filling the balloon with hot gases make it lighter or heavier? If it gets heavier, how does the balloon lift off?

Gravity is a force between objects that pulls them towards each other. It is caused by the mass of the objects, so it is weaker for small objects and stronger for large objects like planets. Gravity acts no matter how far away you are from something, but it gets much weaker as the distance increases. In a hot air balloon you are slightly further from the centre of the Earth, so gravity is slightly smaller and things weigh slightly less. Some hot air balloons can go to over 20 km high, but even at that height gravity is less than 1% weaker than on the ground. Weight is a measure of the force of gravity on an object because of its mass. If gravity is weaker the weight is less, but the mass doesn't change. Mass and weight are easily confused, but they are not the same. Make a table to show how weight and mass compare. Things to include in your table are definitions, how they are measured, units for measuring, whether, where and how they change, and when they are used.

10.14 Does gravity change with height?

Discuss what you know about gravity in different places. For example, do things fall on the top of a mountain? How do things fall on the Moon? How do satellites stay in orbit? What does this tell you about whether and how gravity might change? Check your ideas using a textbook or internet sources. What aspects of our lives would change if gravity didn't exist?

Gravity is a force between objects that pulls them towards each other. It is caused by the mass of the objects, so it is weaker for small objects and stronger for large objects like planets. Gravity acts no matter how far away you are from something, but it gets much weaker as the distance increases. You are a bit further from the centre of the Earth on top of a mountain, so gravity will be slightly weaker – about 0.3% less at the top of Mount Everest. You wouldn't notice this and it would be hard to measure even with very accurate equipment. Objects get more potential energy when they are moved further away from the Earth, against the force of gravity. An object at the top of a mountain has more potential energy than at the bottom. It gets this potential energy as you carry it up to the top, and it's possible to get it back by letting it fall back down the mountain. Use diagrams to explain why it is easier to launch interplanetary spaceships from an orbiting Space Station than from the surface of the Earth.

Earth, space and gravity

10.15 What forces act on orbiters?

Tie an eraser onto a piece of string and whirl it round your head. Talk about how the eraser moves in a circle and what forces must be acting for this to happen. Warn your friends, then let the string go and see what happens. Talk about what forces must be acting. How can you use this as a model to explain how satellites move around the Earth, and what forces must be acting on the satellite?

Satellites orbit the Earth. A force is needed to keep them travelling in an orbit, and gravity is the force that does this. Gravity is a force that pulls objects towards each other. Without this force a satellite would move in a straight line out into space. Satellites travel at exactly the right speed and distance from the Earth to be pulled by gravity and not get closer to the Earth. The gravitational force is enough to make them keep changing direction and travelling in an orbit, but not enough to pull them closer to the ground. They are falling towards the Earth but not getting closer to the Earth. Satellites may have small thruster rockets to make minor adjustments to their movement, but these thruster rockets don't keep them moving in orbit. Use these ideas to explain how the Moon orbits the Earth and the Earth orbits the Sun. Create a poster to illustrate your ideas.

10.16 How do space rockets accelerate?

Review what you already know about forces and movement. Use a science textbook or the internet to find out about Newton's Laws of Motion. Talk about the implications of these for a space rocket blasting off from Earth. Find out about the stages in a space rocket's journey from blasting off to going into orbit around the Earth. If acceleration = force divided by mass, why aren't space rockets much smaller and lighter so they can accelerate more quickly?

A rocket has to accelerate to about 8 000 metres per second (m/s) to escape from the Earth's gravity and go into a low orbit. To do this it has to burn a lot of fuel. Large rockets need several million litres of fuel to launch. The acceleration of the rocket depends directly on two things, its mass and the force that is pushing it. If the force is doubled, the acceleration doubles. If the mass is doubled, the acceleration is halved. As a space rocket burns fuel its mass decreases. However the engines produce the same force, so the acceleration increases because the same force is pushing less mass. Also as it climbs the air becomes less dense, so air resistance is less. This also means the acceleration can increase. The pull from the Earth's gravity does get weaker as the rocket gets higher, but the effect is quite small. Imagine that you are involved in planning a mission to Mars. Present a case for building and launching a rocket from the International Space Station rather than from the surface of the Earth.

190

References:

Alexander R. (2006) *Towards dialogic teaching.* York: Dialogos.

Black, P. and Wiliam, D. (1998) *Inside the black box.* Kings College, London.

Black, P. and Harrison, C. (2004) *Science inside the black box.* NferNelson, London.

Black, P., Harrison, C., Lee C., Marshall B. and Wiliam D. (2002) *Working inside the black box.* Kings College, London.

Keogh, B. and Naylor, S. (1999) Concept Cartoons, teaching and learning in science: an evaluation. *International Journal of Science Education,* 21 (4) 431-446.

Naylor, S. and Keogh, B. (2007) Active Assessment: thinking, learning and assessment in science. *School Science Review,* 88 (325) 73-79.

Naylor, S., Keogh, B. and Goldsworthy, A. (2004) *Active Assessment: thinking, learning and assessment in science.* Sandbach: Millgate House Publishers.

White, R. and Gunstone, R. (1992) *Probing understanding.* London: Falmer.

References to research into Concept Cartoons

Chin, C. and Teou L.Y. (2009) Using Concept Cartoons in formative assessment: scaffolding students' argumentation. *International Journal of Science Education*, 31, 10, 1307-1332.

Downing, B. (2005) *Developing the nature and the role of quality argument in primary science lessons through the use of Concept Cartoons.* Unpublished PhD thesis, Manchester Metropolitan University.

Education Extra (1998) *Science on the Underground: An evaluation of the Concept Cartoon project by Education Extra.* London: Education Extra.

Ekici, F., Ekici, E. and Aydin, F. (2007) Utility of Concept Cartoons in diagnosing and overcoming misconceptions related to photosynthesis. *International Journal of Science Education*, 2, 4,111-124.

Kabapinar, F. (2005) Effectiveness of teaching via Concept Cartoons from the point of view of constructivist approach. *Educational Sciences: Theory and Practice*, 5,1,135-146.

Keogh, B. and Naylor, S. (1993) Learning in science: another way in. *Primary Science Review*, 26, 22-23.

Keogh, B. (1995) An exploration of the possible value of cartoons as a teaching approach in science. *Unpublished MA dissertation*, Manchester Metropolitan University.

Keogh, B. and Naylor, S. (1996) Learning in science: cartoons as an innovative teaching and learning approach. In K. Calhoun, R. Panwar and S. Shrum (Eds.) *Proceedings of the 8th Symposium of the International Organisation of Science and Technology Education*, Vol 3, 133-9. Edmonton, Canada.

Keogh, B. and Naylor, S. (1997) Making sense of constructivism in the classroom. *Science Teacher Education*, 20, 12-14.

Keogh, B. and Naylor, S. (1997) Developing children's ideas: putting constructivism into practice in teacher education. In R. Feasey (Ed.) *Proceedings of the third summer conference for teacher education in primary science*, 139-146. University of Durham, UK.

Keogh, B. and Naylor, S. (1998) Teaching and Learning in Science using Concept Cartoons. *Primary Science Review*, 51, 14-16.

Keogh B and Naylor S (1999), Concept Cartoons, teaching and learning in science: an evaluation. *International Journal of Science Education*, 21,4,431-446.

Keogh B. & Naylor S. (2000) Teaching and learning in science using Concept Cartoons: why Dennis wants to stay in at playtime. *Investigating* 16, 3, 10-14.

Keogh B. & Naylor S. (2000) Concept Cartoons and issues in science teacher education. *Proceedings of the SCIcentre/ASET conference 2000*, 108-112. Leicester.

Keogh, B., Naylor, S. and Wilson, C. (1998) Concept Cartoons: a new perspective on physics education. *Physics Education*, 33, 4, 219-224.

Kinchin, I. (2000) Concept mapping activities to help students understand photosynthesis – and teachers understand students. *School Science Review*, 82 (299), 11-14.

Millar, L. and Murdoch, J. (2002) A penny for your thoughts. *Primary Science Review*, 72, 26-9.

Morris, M. Merritt, M., Fairclough, S., Birrell, N. and Howitt. C. (2007) Trialling Concept Cartoons in early childhood teaching and learning of science. *Teaching Science*.

Naylor, S. and Keogh, B. (1999), Constructivism in the Classroom: Theory into Practice. *Journal of Science Teacher Education*, 10(2) 93-106.

Naylor, S. and Keogh, B. (1999), Science on the Underground: an initial evaluation. *Public Understanding of Science*, 8, 1-18.

Naylor S. and Keogh B. (2000) *Concept Cartoons in Science Education*. Sandbach: Millgate House Publishers.

Naylor, S., Keogh, B., de Boo, M. and Feasey, R. (2000) Researching formative assessment: Concept Cartoons as an auditing strategy. In R.Duit (Ed.) *Research in Science Education: Past, Present and Future*. Dordrecht: Kluwer.

Naylor S. and Keogh B. (2002) Concept Cartoons. *Teaching thinking*, 9, 8-12.

Naylor S., Keogh B. and Downing, B. (2003) Argumentation in the primary science classroom. *Science Teacher Education*, 35, 3-5.

Naylor S., Keogh B. and Downing, B. (2007) Argumentation and primary science. *Research in Science Education*, 37, 17-39.

Oluk, S. and Ozalp, I. (2007) The teaching of global environmental problems according to the constructivist approach: as a focal point of the problem and the availability of Concept Cartoons. *Educational Sciences Theory and Practice*, 7, 2, 881-896.

References

Rahmat, F. A. (2009). Use of Concept Cartoons as a strategy to address pupils' misconceptions in primary four science topic on matter. In A. L. Tan, H. M. Wong, & S., Tan (Eds.), *Action research: Empowering my practice in teaching science* (pp. 11-37). Singapore: National Institute of Education and Science Exploria, East Zone Centre of Excellence for Primary Science.

Stephenson P. and Warwick P. (2002) Using Concept Cartoons to support progression in students' understanding of light. *Physics Education, 37,* 2, 135-141.

Concept Cartoon and Active Assessment publications

Dabell, J. (2006) *Thinking about maths* poster set. Sandbach: Millgate House Publishers.

Dabell, J., Keogh, B. and Naylor, S. (2008) *Concept Cartoons in mathematics education.* Sandbach: Millgate House Publishers.

Keogh, B. and Naylor, S. (1997) *Starting points for science.* Sandbach: Millgate House Publishers.

Keogh, B. and Naylor, S. (1997) *Thinking about science* poster set. Sandbach: Millgate House Publishers.

Keogh, B. and Naylor, S. (1999) *Thinking about science 2* poster set. Sandbach: Millgate House Publishers.

Keogh, B., Dabell, J. and Naylor, S. (2008) *Active Assessment: thinking, learning and assessment in English.* Sandbach: Millgate House Publishers.

Keogh, B., Dabell, J. and Naylor, S. (2010) *Active Assessment: thinking, learning and assessment in mathematics.* Sandbach: Millgate House Publishers.

Keogh, B. & Naylor, S. (2006, 2007) Spellbound Science 1 and 2. Millgate House Publishers.

Naylor, S. and Keogh, B. (2000) *Concept Cartoons in science education.* Sandbach: Millgate House Publishers.

References

Naylor, S., Keogh, B. and Goldsworthy, A. (2004) *Active Assessment: thinking, learning and assessment in science.* Sandbach: Millgate House Publishers.

Naylor, S. and Naylor, B. (2000) *Science Questions books series.* London, Hodder Children's Books. Now available from Millgate House Publishers. Published by Millgate House Publishers on CD ROM (2009)